NOGALES

LIFE AND TIMES ON THE FRONTIER

In 1923, General Alvaro Obregón presented the Nogales Arizona Chamber of Commerce with a beautiful handwoven serape. (Courtesy Pimería Alta Historical Society.)

THE
MAKING OF AMERICA
SERIES

NOGALES
LIFE AND TIMES ON THE FRONTIER

JANE EPPINGA
PIMERIA ALTA HISTORICAL SOCIETY

ARCADIA
PUBLISHING

Published by Arcadia Publishing
Charleston SC, Chicago IL, Portsmouth NH, San Francisco CA

For all general information contact Arcadia Publishing at:
Telephone 843-853-2070
Fax 843-853-0044
E-Mail sales@arcadiapublishing.com
For customer service and orders:
Toll-Free 1-888-313-2665

Visit us on the Internet at www.arcadiapublishing.com

FRONT COVER: *The Ruby posse captured Placido Silvas and Manuel Martinez for the murders of Frank Pearson and his wife in 1921. Martinez was executed in 1923, but Silvas escaped and was never recaptured. (Courtesy Pimería Alta Historical Society.)*

CONTENTS

ACKNOWLEDGMENTS

The work of the book is never entirely the work of one person and so it is with *Nogales: Life and Times on the Frontier*. Many individuals have helped the author, including Sigrid Maitrejean, J. Eduardo Robinson, Axel Holm, and Teresa Leal from the Pimería Alta Historical Society. Abe Rochlin, Fred Rochlin, Harriet Rochlin, and Abe Chanin provided material on early Jewish pioneers in Nogales. Paul Allen of the *Tucson Citizen* put me in contact with Cabot Sedgwick, who does much to save historical sites in Nogales. Mary Bingham of the Tubac Historical Society provided pictures and sources. Virginia Culin Roberts shared her material on Larcena Pennington. Pat Stephenson shared her knowledge of Tom and Louise Marshall. Organizations which have contributed to this work are the National Archives in Washington, D.C., Library of Congress, Arizona Historical Society, Arizona State Archives, and the Pimería Alta Historical Society. Thanks also to two venerable California Institutions: The Bancroft Library at Berkeley and The Huntington Library in San Merino. Thanks also to Jim Kempert and the fine staff at Arcadia Publishing. Finally, no one made more important contributions than those pioneers who left their stories and mark on Nogales and Santa Cruz County.

INTRODUCTION

On March 15, 1899 Arizona's smallest county (Santa Cruz, at 797,240 acres), was carved out of parts of Pima and Cochise Counties, with Nogales as the seat of the new county's government. Two names, Papago and Grant, had been proposed for the new county, but these were discarded in favor Santa Cruz, which means "the blessed cross." The name was taken from the Santa Cruz River that traversed the county, for what can be more important in a desert than the life-sustaining flow of water that promises survival.

One of the richest silver mines ever discovered, the Real de Arizonac, gave Arizona its name. Nogales took its name from the grove of walnuts (nogales) found there.

Santa Cruz County encompasses lands explored by Spanish conquistadores who sought to claim the land for the Spanish crown and Spanish priests who hoped to gain souls for the realm of God. They called this land the Pimería Alta, "upper Pima lands," after the large number of Pima Indians inhabiting the area. In the vicinity of Nogales, the first black man known to enter the region, Estevan, crossed from what was New Spain into what is now Arizona probably in the area of Lochiel. Closely following him was Fray Marcos de Niza on his search for the seven cities of Cibola reputed to be of pure gold.

As the land transferred from Spain to Mexico and ultimately to the United States, a boundary between Mexico and Arizona had to be drawn and what could be more germane to the making of America than the establishment of one of its borders? Over the years, the people who gathered in the grove of walnuts around Monument 122 on both sides of the border preserved their own very distinct culture as they conducted business, intermarried, and at times fought with each other. The two towns of Nogales, Arizona and its sister city, Nogales, Sonora, Mexico are often referred to as Ambos Nogales, or "both Nogales."

After the Spanish explorations, emigrants rushed to California to take part in that national insanity, the 1849 California gold rush. These people left their imprint on history and many returned to Nogales and Tucson after their disappointment in California. Travel went east and west but also north and south. Nogales, the largest port of entry city within Arizona, continues to witness passage between Mexico and the United States. Not only do people pass this way, but billions of pounds of fruits and vegetables cross the border here to grace tables in the United States.

Santa Cruz County stretches for only 60 miles along the international border and extends only 30 miles to the north. Yet, it has witnessed important events in history, such as the Mexican Revolution, and has been visited by presidents from both countries. Historic forts, including Crittenden and Buchanan, were established here to protect pioneer settlers and famous ranches were established by men such as Pete Kitchen. However, it was El Dorado, the lure for gold and mineral wealth on both sides of the border, which drew the settlers. Merchants and ranchers in turn made money supplying the military and miners with foods and material goods.

Nogales, which began with a peddler's shack in the desert, in a few short years became a seat of government. Over the years, it has had more than its fair share of problems. Drug smuggling has reached epidemic proportions. Illegal immigrants cross the border daily to try to find work in the United States, but many find death from thirst in an inhospitable desert. Yet, these resilient people on both sides of the border continue to survive with an unsurpassed flair for life and living.

This site on the William Barnett Ranch is where the Real de Arizonac was located about 25 miles south of Nogales. (Courtesy Alma Ready.)

1. THOSE WHO CAME BEFORE

Nogales, the county seat of Arizona's smallest county, Santa Cruz, looks back on its history with pride and forward with hope. Patagonia, Santa Cruz County's only other incorporated town, along with Sonoita and Elgin are still traditional ranching communities, but are gaining renown for their wineries. Oro Blanco, Ruby, Harshaw, Washington Camp, and Mowry echo with the whispers of ghosts telling a colorful history. Tubac, Tumacácori, and Calabasas have deep roots in the Spanish conquest for the cross and the crown. Santa Cruz County may be small, but it covers approximately 60 miles of an international border where people, law abiding and criminal, and merchandise, legal and contraband, pass back and forth between Mexico and the United States.

Long before an international border separated Mexico and the United States, a river flowed, providing sustenance for life for a prehistoric people. The Santa Cruz River—river of the Holy Cross—meanders from Tucson, Arizona, into Mexico, and then back again into Santa Cruz County. Once, this river had flowing water year round, but now its banks overflow only during the monsoons.

Long before the Spanish conquistadores Francisco Coronado and Juan Bautista de Anza, and Spanish priests Fray Marcos de Niza and Padre Eusebio Kino, explored this land, ancient civilizations had already left their mark. About 11,000 years before a few merchants set up their stores in a grove of Nogales or walnut trees, nomadic people hunted Ice Age mammals. Archaeologists named one group after their beautifully crafted Clovis arrowheads that were first identified in Clovis, New Mexico. These Clovis hunters, with their distinctive projectiles, followed the mammoth, mastodon, horse, bison, and tapir at several Arizona sites until the close of the last Ice Age. Clovis hunters faced danger in spearing an adult mammoth, which stood more than 12 feet tall and weighed more than 10,000 pounds. The Clovis people herded groups of mammoths over the cliffs, resulting in the wasteful slaughter of many animals, but affording themselves a safer hunt.

In 1951, the bones of an extinct mammoth with eight spear points in its head and ribs were discovered on the United States side of the border. A few years later, the remains of nine mammoths were found on the Lehner Ranch on the banks of the San Pedro River.

When Fray Pedro Font visited the Nogales area with Captain Juan Bautista de Anza in 1775, he wrote that they stopped at a place known as Las Lagunas and that this land was abundant in pasturage. Nogales is home to this very small wetlands still known as Las Lagunas. This 4-acre site has been kept pristine by its owner, 89-year-old Cabot Sedgwick, a longtime Nogales resident and former Foreign Service officer. Because Las Lagunas sits on a table of relatively impermeable material, runoff water is collected during the rainy season and the soil never dries up, making it a popular habitat for birds and mammals. Las Lagunas was home to the Hohokam Indians between 100 and 1200 A.D. Approximately a dozen families left evidence of their residence in the form of pottery shards.

The Hohokam, ancient ancestors of the modern Pima and Tohono o'odham (Papago) tribes, inhabited Arizona from 1 B.C. to 1400 A.D. They cremated their

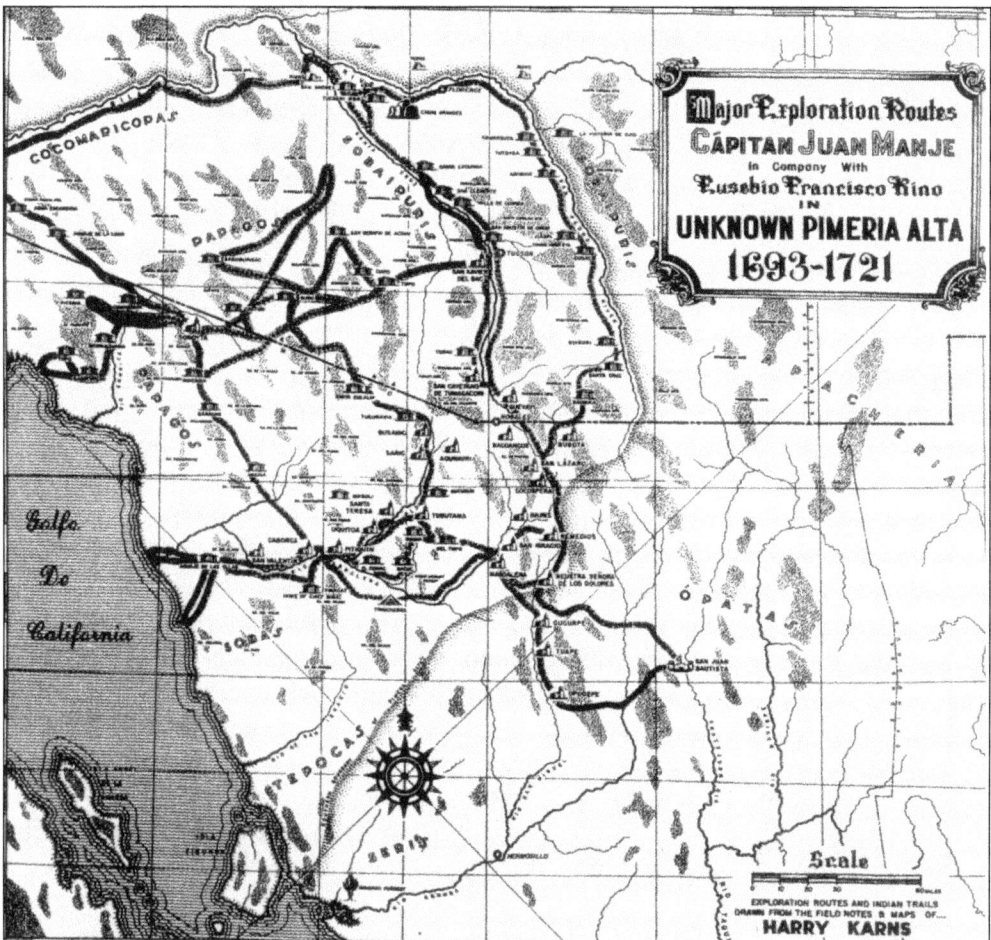

Captain Juan Manje mapped these major exploration routes in the company of Father Eusebio Francisco Kino, an Italian missionary who served on the Pimería Alta for almost 47 years. (Courtesy Cabot Sedgewick.)

dead, leaving no skeletal remains from which archaeologists could determine their physical appearance. They did leave evidence, however, that they were excellent artisans in clay and stone, and they made axes with wooden handles.

Hohokam villages contained ball courts and platform mounds like the Mayas and Incas of Central and South America, and they played a form of basketball with the rings set vertically in the court walls. As their population increased, larger villages appeared and artifacts from their roasting pits reflect their knowledge of processing and cooking plants and animals. The presence of grinding stones suggests that these people had become dependent on wild grains, nuts, and roots for food and medicine.

The Hohokam grew corn to supplement cactus fruits and their agriculture required the construction of intricate gravity-fed irrigation systems. Known as the Masters of the Desert, the Hohokam irrigation systems consisted of more than 200 miles of canals. Their reservoirs impounded water, which enabled year-round crop growing. They also dug wells to intercept the shallow ground water, which they diverted and allocated via canals to other villages. Excavation and maintenance of reservoirs required organized labor and the subsequent centralization of authority. During their final period from 1200 to 1400 A.D., the Hohokam may have been invaded by Pueblo tribes. What happened to the Hohokam is still a matter of conjecture. Perhaps their lands no longer sustained farming or they may have become integrated with other tribes.

In 1966, a University of Arizona archaeological team discovered what may have been another civilization about 100 miles southwest of Nogales. The Trincheras, dating from approximately 200 to 1450 A.D., lived in the Altar Valley of Sonora, Mexico. The Trincheras culture may have begun with separate traditions from the Hohokam and later integrated with the Hohokam. Their colorful pottery suggested that they may have been farmers and foragers who lived in shallow pit houses. The village of Trincheras in Mexico continues to be inhabited and its hillsides are covered with artificial terraces.

Spaniards began their explorations in the mid-1500s and fortunately left extensive diaries describing the people they encountered in the New World. Spanish soldiers and priests found the Tohono o'odham, Pimas, and Apaches living along the Santa Cruz River banks.

Fray Marcos de Niza, born in Nice in the Duchy of Savoy, entered the Franciscan order around 1531. As both priest and explorer, he served in Central America and Peru before being transferred to Mexico City in 1537. A year later, Viceroy Antonio de Mendoza entrusted De Niza with investigating rumors of enormous riches on the frontiers of New Spain. De Niza was described as:

> a regular priest, pious, endowed with all virtues and dedication, was approved and recognized as capable of making this journey of discovery, not only because of the qualities indicated above, but also because of his knowledge of theology, cosmography and navigation.

11

De Niza may have been the first European to explore what is today southern Arizona when he crossed the land near Lochiel east of Nogales. He was preceded by his scout and guide Estevan, a dark-skinned Moorish slave, who had served Alvar Nuñez Cabeza de Vaca. De Vaca had reported stories of the seven cities of Cibola, which were supposed to be made of gold. Despite his eight-year journeys with De Vaca, De Niza, and his owner Andres Dorantes, during which he endured periods of hunger and danger, Estevan's slave status never changed. The viceroy, in his report to the king, wrote that he had retained a "Negro" to guide Fray Marcos. In his instruction to De Niza, the viceroy admonished Estevan to obey the priests.

De Niza, Estevan, a lay brother, and several Native Americans who carried the expedition's supplies, left Culiacán in March 1539. Along the way, many women fell in love with handsome Estevan. When he reached the Zuni villages of New Mexico, the Zuni men, who had no intention of permitting him to work his charm on their women, descended on him with a hail of arrows. One of the Indians escaped and told De Niza a horrible tale of carnage and death. When the rest of the Indians refused to continue, De Niza was forced to hurry back to Mexico City.

De Niza told the viceroy that he had seen the golden cities of Cibola, but he had only observed the Zuni villages from a distance, which appear to be golden in the sunset. On the basis of the priest's report, the viceroy launched another expedition under Francisco de Coronado with De Niza as a guide. When Coronado reached Zuni in July 1540, the disappointed explorer denounced De Niza as a liar. The disgraced priest returned to Mexico City where he suffered the scorn of the military until his death on March 25, 1558.

Almost a century later, Padre Eusebio Kino arrived on the Rim of Christendom. Kino, born on August 10, 1645, in Segno, Italy, suffered as a youth from a raging fever. When doctors despaired of his life, Kino promised his patron saint, San Francisco Xavier, that if his life were spared, he would become a missionary. Kino recovered and entered the Jesuit order. Upon his arrival in Mexico, he secured a royal decree freeing Indian converts for 20 years from compulsory mine labor. The decree endeared Kino to the natives and facilitated his work.

This hard-riding Jesuit arrived in the Santa Cruz River area in early 1690 and a delegation of Pimas from Tumacácori invited the priest to visit their homes. Kino gathered his congregations from the scattered Pima tribes and built his churches on the Pimería Alta, which covered more than 50,000 square miles of southern Arizona and northern Sonora. Kino's understanding of human frailty and his sense of humor enabled him to cope with the frustration, danger, and loneliness of the Frontier. He labored not only as a priest but also as a cartographer, trader, rancher, explorer, and architect. About 10 miles north of the international border, Kino established a ranchería, which taught the Pimas the principles of ranching and farming, while at the same time caring for their souls. The magnificent San Xavier del Bac near Tucson, the Tumacácori mission, and Guevavi near Nogales are three remnants of Kino's Arizona work.

Baroness Suzanne Silvercruys sculpted this statue of Father Eusebio Francisco Kino, which stands in front of the Arizona Historical Society. Another statue from this mold is in the National Hall of Statuary in Washington, D.C.

Together with his friend Padre Agustín Campos, Kino served on the Pimería Alta for almost 47 years, and founded a chain of missions within a 200-mile radius of Nogales. They mastered seven Pima dialects and established a training school at San Ignacio for Jesuits working on the frontier.

Tubac had been established as a presidio to house the soldiers and protect Spain's interests. On October 23, 1775, Captain Juan Bautista de Anza left Tubac with a party of 240 men and 1,000 livestock and horses to make his famous overland trek across the desert to the Pacific Ocean to establish the Presidio of San Francisco.

13

Juan Bautista de Anza II, graduate of the College of Royal Engineers in Mexico City and commander of the Tubac Presidio, traveled across the desert to establish the Presidio of San Francisco. (Courtesy California Historical Society.)

The recording of the first civilian land grant to Torrivio de Otero in Santa Cruz County has been preserved. In the late 1790s, Lieutenant Nicolas de Errán wrote about the poignant ceremony on the frontier:

> Whereas the resident Torrivio de Otero has presented himself to me, petitioning for a house lot on which to establish himself in this Presidio and in consideration of the benefit resulting from the establishment of an industrious settler, such as the petitioner, who will cultivate the soil, thereby furnishing a supply of grain, which, in some seasons has to be brought in from a long distance. I therefore by authority conferred on me by the King (Spain) grant to the said Torrivio de Otero, and donate to him as a first settler, perpetually, forever the right of inheritance to him and his children and descendants, a lot on which to build his house on the lower side of the Presidio in the direction of the south, with a front to the north of twenty varas and as a tract of land for cultivation distant from the presidio about one-eight of a league.
>
> . . . And the said Torrivio de Otero being informed of the foregoing, I took him by the hand and gave his possession of said lands, he according to the custom scattering earth and stone and pulling up herbiage.

Otero understood that he would be required to keep arms and horses and be ever ready to defend the country against enemies.

On September 18, 1958, the Tubac Presidio State Historical Park was formally dedicated in the presence of the mayors of Nogales, Arizona; Nogales, Sonora; and Tucson along with other dignitaries. Tubac, with much of Arizona's oldest history, became the state's first historical monument. In 1974, University of Arizona archaeologists excavated portions of the presidio and two years later, an underground archaeological display provided visitors with views of the original foundations, walls, and floor of the commandant's quarters as well as artifacts of Tubac's history. Tourists may also visit the old schoolhouse and Otero community hall, which are on the National Register of Historic Places. In October, the accomplishments of De Anza are commemorated during Anza days.

Tumacácori National Historic Park is located on 45 acres in three separate units. San Jose de Tumacácori and Los Santa Angeles de Guevavi are the two oldest missions in Arizona. The third unit, San Cayetano de Calabasas, was established in 1756. Visits to the Guevavi and Calabasas sites are by reservation only during the monthly tours guided by the park staff. Tumacácori was designated a national monument on September 15, 1908 and created as a national historical park on August 6, 1990.

Mission San José del Tumacácori Mission is now under the aegis of the National Park Service. Now a national historic park, the mission is open to visitors, who can view artifacts and original foundations of the missions.

2. THE LINE IS DRAWN

When the U.S. Boundary Commission drew the "Line" between Mexico and the United States, it passed through Los Nogales Pass. Monuments 121 and 122 mark the border separating Nogales, Arizona and Nogales, Sonora, Mexico. The 2,000-mile-long boundary snaking through the deserts of California, Arizona, New Mexico, and Texas separates national property, but it could never separate the people who, with their social needs, move back and forth across the land and share their cultures. The early remoteness of the area forced English-speaking pioneers to form bonds of friendship, often cemented in marriage, with their Spanish-speaking neighbors. More often than not, the area is referred to as La Frontera, "the frontier" and the sister cities of Nogales, Sonora and Nogales, Arizona are together known simply as Ambos Nogales, "both Nogales."

Four men—John Russell Bartlett, James Gadsden, Andrew Belcher Gray, and William H. Emory—played important roles in establishing the United States–Mexico border. John Russell Bartlett, a Manhattan bookseller, with no experience in topography or surveying, was appointed survey commissioner on June 15, 1850. James Gadsden, a railroad man, negotiated the purchase of southern Arizona from Mexico in 1853. Andrew Belcher Gray surveyed the border to determine the best site to build the transcontinental railroad. And in 1846, Major William H. Emory accompanied the Army of the West on its 2,000-mile western trek to collect scientific, economic, and geographic information on the American Southwest. He started from Bent's Fort in Colorado, traveled through New Mexico and Arizona, and finished in San Diego. In July of 1851, Emory reported that the survey had been completed and that all of the monuments were in place.

During the 1840s, many Americans were against drawing any line separating the United States from the rest of the continent. The *New York Morning News* wrote, "Our way lies not over trampled nations, but through desert wastes." However, many more wanted to acquire all of Mexico, including James K. Polk of Tennessee, who won the 1844 presidential election by a narrow margin. His were the politics of Manifest Destiny and the annexation of as much land as possible. Mexico's President Antonio Lopez de Santa Anna notified the United States that annexation of Mexico's lands would be "equivalent to a declaration of a war." When Polk assumed the presidency in 1845, Congress voted to admit Texas to the Union and Mexico severed diplomatic relations with the United States. Polk, spoiling for a war, announced that Mexico had invaded lands belonging to the United States and Congress declared war on Mexico on April 13, 1846. By the end of the year, the American military controlled most of New Mexico, which included present-day Arizona, invaded Vera Cruz, and marched on toward Mexico City. The Mexicans fought intensely and American soldiers retaliated. General Winfield Scott wrote that he had seen "atrocities to make Heaven weep and every American of Christian morals blush for his country." In September, the Americans stormed the palace of Chapaultepec, captured Mexico City, and forced the surrender of Mexico.

When peace was restored, the task remained to draw the boundary between the two countries. The assignment would be fulfilled by the U.S. Boundary Survey led by Commissioners John Russell Bartlett for the United States and Pedro García-Condé of Mexico. Bartlett had neither diplomatic nor engineering experience, but he was a loyal Whig and through political machination, he secured his appointment as U.S. commissioner. His appointment came only after the Whigs removed the nomination of Ohio Congressman John J. Weller, and the future Arizona Territorial Governor John C. Frémont turned down his nomination to accept a draft to become one of California's first senators.

John R. Bartlett, a loyal Whig, became the first U.S. Boundary Commissioner in 1850 so he could travel and see Native Americans. His most famous accomplishment was Bartlett's Quotations. *(Courtesy National Archives.)*

Bartlett, born on October 23, 1805 in Providence, Rhode Island to Smith and Nancy Russell Bartlett, moved to Kingston, Ontario where he received a public school education. At Lowville Academy in upstate New York, he studied accounting, history, and literature, and excelled as an artist. In 1824, he returned to Providence to clerk in a dry-goods store and learn banking. Twelve years later, he moved to New York City where he and Charles Welford opened a bookstore that sold literary and scientific publications. Bartlett and Welford's became a gathering place for intellectuals. Bartlett, a founding father of the American Ethnological Society, wrote *The Progress of Ethnology*. His most famous work, *Dictionary of Americanisms*, evolved into *Bartlett's Quotations*.

On June 15, 1850, despite his ignorance of surveying, Bartlett accepted the post of U.S. Boundary Commissioner because he wanted to travel and see Indians. He left New York with a large party on August 3, 1850 and landed at Indianola, Texas 27 days later. After traveling overland, he arrived at El Paso to begin work with his Mexican counterpart, Pedro García-Condé. The surveyors found it difficult to establish their starting point along the southern boundary of New Mexico along the Rio Grande, because of inaccuracies in Disturnell's 1847 Map of the United Mexican States. Bartlett allowed the boundary to be set 42 miles north of El Paso. When surveyor Andrew B. Gray refused to agree to this, Bartlett set out for a tour of northwestern Mexico. When the work was complete, Congress rejected the Bartlett–García Condé line.

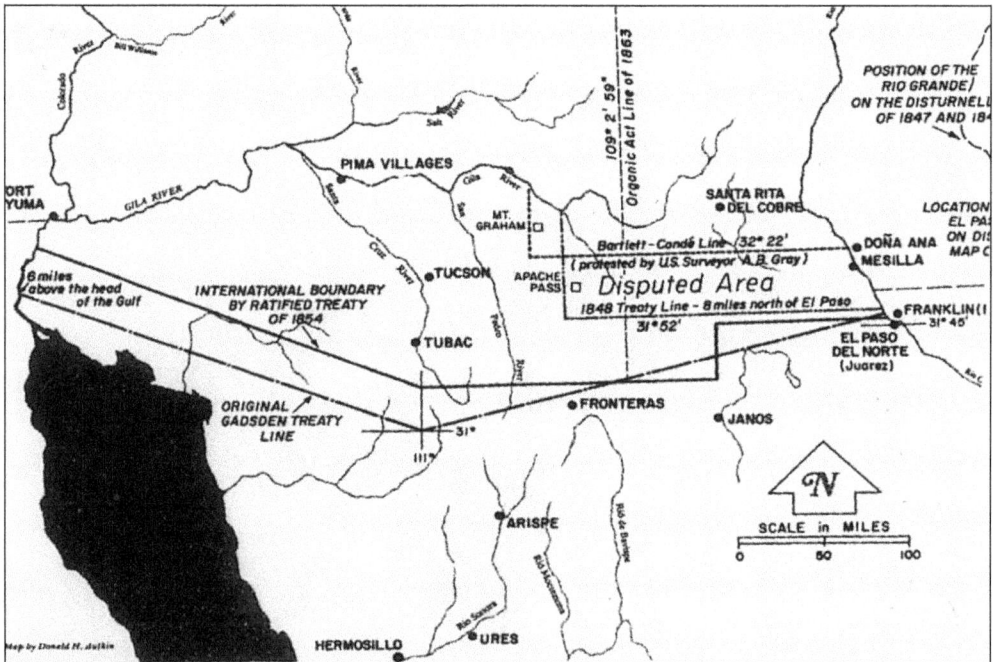

This map of the disputed area that led to the Gadsden Purchase illustrates the desert land that the United States desired for the transcontinental railroad. (Courtesy Don Bufkin.)

General Pedro García Condé, born at Arizpe, Sonora in 1806, joined the Mexican army at the age of 12. In 1844, he became Secretary of War and Marine and four years later was elected to the national senate. García Condé so strongly believed in the border survey work that he often paid his crew out of his own pocket when government monies were not forthcoming. His father had served as the Spanish military governor of the northwest inland provinces and his son became a cadet in the regiment of Cerro-Gordo in Durango in 1817. In 1835, García Condé took part in the campaign against Texas and after the defeat of Santa Anna, he was appointed inspector-general of the militia. On June 30, 1838, he was appointed director of the military college, a post he held until 1844. Three years later, the State of Sonora elected General García-Condé to congress. As Secretary of War, he began reorganizing the army, but before he could complete this work, a new revolution overthrew the government. Mexico's war with the United States began while García-Condé was in exile in Chihuahua. When he offered his services, he was appointed commander of the cavalry on the northwestern frontier.

Because of Bartlett's error, the U.S. Congress negotiated the Gadsden Purchase in 1853, which transferred inhospitable desert lands to the United States, but was viewed as essential for establishing a southern route for the transcontinental railroad. Bartlett returned to Rhode Island and wrote a two-volume *Personal Narrative of Explorations and Incidents in Texas, New Mexico, California, Sonora, and Chihuahua, Connected with the United States and Mexican Boundary Commission, during the years 1850, 51, 52, and 53* (1854), which became a standard source of information on the Southwest. From 1855 to 1872, he served as Rhode Island Secretary of State. He helped amass the collection of boundary information that constitutes the nucleus of the John Carter Brown Library and he published a *Bibliography of Rhode Island, Records of the Colony of Rhode Island and Providence Plantation, The Literature of Rebellion, Bibliographic Notices of Rare and Curious Books Relating to America in the Library of John Carter Brown, Letters of Roger Williams,* and *Letters of Roger Williams to Winthrop,* in addition to various monographs and bibliographies. Bartlett died on May 28, 1886 in Providence, Rhode Island. Although he frustrated engineers, incurred the wrath of the governments of two countries, and saw his work disavowed by President Millard Filmore, he had fixed his "magisterial gaze" upon this land and left us a wonderful legacy of life along the border. Bartlett had authorized the spending of almost a half-million dollars, but only about $100,000 was actually spent on marking the boundary.

Knowing that Mexico's coffers were almost empty, President James Polk hired James Gadsden to negotiate the sale of the land that today includes Nogales. Gadsden, born in 1788, was a grandson of Christopher Gadsden, a South Carolina Revolutionary soldier who had been captured by the British at Charleston. Gadsden was no stranger to politics. President James Monroe appointed and charged him as Indian Commissioner with responsibility of placing Florida's Seminole Indians on reservations. Gadsden became interested in promoting railroads and, upon his return to South Carolina in 1839, was chosen

Before negotiating the purchase of lands, which include present-day Nogales, with Mexico, James Gadsden was appointed Indian Commissioner by President James Monroe. (Courtesy National Archives.)

president of the South Carolina Railroad Company. He wanted to connect all Southern railroads into one system and then to connect this system with the transcontinental railroad to the Pacific. This would make the West commercially dependent on the South instead of the North.

After engineers advised Gadsden that the most direct and practicable route for the southern transcontinental railroad would be south of the boundary established by Bartlett, he drew up plans to have the federal government acquire title to the necessary territory from Mexico. President Franklin Pierce appointed Gadsden as Minister Plenipotentiary and Envoy Extraordinary with instructions to persuade President Antonio Lopéz de Santa Anna to accept $10 million and acquire enough territory from Mexico for a railroad to the Gulf of California.

Mexico was already bitter with the signing of the Treaty Guadalupe-Hidalgo on February 2, 1848. It had lost its claim to Texas and ceded to the United States New Mexico, Arizona, California, Colorado, Utah, and Nevada along with parts of Wyoming, Kansas, Colorado, and Oklahoma. In return, the United States had paid Mexico $15 million and assumed responsibility for paying $3 million in claims by American citizens against the Mexican government for Apache depredations.

The United States wanted to make boundary adjustments, and Gadsden wanted a railroad route. Mexico needed money and wanted a settlement of its Indian claims against the United States. Gadsden agreed to pay Santa Anna $10 million for approximately 30,000 acres of land south of the Gila River in what is now southwestern New Mexico and southern Arizona. Gadsden did not live to see the Southern Pacific Railroad built through his purchase. In the hazy area of what might have been, when the inhabitants of Arizona petitioned Congress for a territorial government in 1854, one of the names suggested for the new territory was Gadsdonia.

Neither Mexico nor the United States was satisfied with Gadsden's purchase. The deal so angered the Mexicans that Santa Anna was banished, but not before he skimmed off about 25 percent of the Gadsden Purchase monies for personal use. Bartlett's work was taken over by surveyor Andrew B. Gray, who assumed his duties after an eight-month delay that included his own illness. Andrew Belcher Gray was born on July 6, 1820 in Norfolk, Virginia where his father William Gray served as the British Consul. After Gray helped Captain Andrew Talcott survey the Mississippi River delta, Edwin W. Moore recruited him and his brother Alfred into the Texas Navy. Gray, not one to hold his temper, was reputed to have shot and wounded another boundary commissioner, Colonel John B. Weller, in San Diego.

Andrew Gray's boundary work began at San Diego, where boundary marker 1 was established. He, too, pointed out that Disturnell's map was faulty and that the United States stood to lose valuable land if it was used. Bartlett admitted that

U.S. Border Monument 122 was enveloped by John Brickwood's Exchange Saloon. (Courtesy Library of Congress.)

the map was incorrect, but hoped that it would be corrected during the surveying process. At stake was the very land that Gray considered the only practicable southern railroad route to the Pacific. Gray protested that Bartlett's line was too far north and his disagreement with Bartlett became so bitter that Gray was replaced by William H. Emory. At stake were 6,000 square miles south of Arizona's Gila River that Bartlett insisted could "never be inhabited." Oh, if he could see us now! Gray did not disagree, but he wanted the land for the transcontinental railway and completed his survey.

Gray explored Tubac, Tucson, and the Nogales area near the famous Real de Arizonac, with its once-fabulous silver mines. He subsequently published his report on the Mexican boundary survey, *Survey of a Route for the Southern Pacific Railroad, on the 32nd Parallel* (1856). During his years prior to the Civil War, Gray resided in Tucson, where he surveyed government properties and was appointed to the Office of Indian Affairs to mark the newly established Pima/Papago (now Tohono o'odham) reservation.

About a week after the battle of Shiloh in 1862, 42-year-old Captain Andrew Belcher Gray was working on maps in a steamer cabin plying its way along the Mississippi River near the Arkansas shore just below Fort Pillow. An explosion blew up a boiler plate, spewing timber fragments and scalding steam, killing Gray.

Surveyor Andrew Belcher Gray, while working on the U.S.-Mexico boundary commission, had serious disagreements with Bartlett. Their differences of opinion caused Belcher to be replaced by Emory. (Courtesy National Archives.)

Major William Hemsley Emory, an 1831 graduate of the United States Military Academy at West Point, served his country in a military capacity, but is best known for his work as a topographical engineer. His 1853–1854 explorations and subsequent publications established him as an authority on the West.

Born on September 11, 1811 to Thomas and Anna Maria Hemsley Emory in Queen Anne's County, Maryland, Emory was a third-generation soldier. His grandfather was a veteran of the American Revolution and his father Thomas fought in the War of 1812. The Emorys had immigrated from Great Britain in the eighteenth century and acquired patent property from the Lord Proprietor of Maryland. Through prudent management and the latest farming techniques, their farm became a showcase southern estate.

Early in 1823, his father obtained an appointment for 11-year-old William to attend West Point through his friend and business acquaintance, South Carolina statesman John C. Calhoun. The Emory family also counted among their close friends Jefferson Davis and Henry Clay Jr. Because the Emorys shipped their thoroughbreds to the Clays, who then transported the horses down the Mississippi River for sale in New Orleans, young Henry Clay and William Emory spent considerable time together in Kentucky.

At the United States Military Academy at West Point, their childhood friendship grew when William joined the class of 1827. Here, William began growing the long sideburns which eventually developed into flamboyant, mutton-chop whiskers. Along with earning a reputation as a daredevil, Emory studied hard and devoted himself to scientific subjects. Despite his love of science, he never forgot his primary reason for attending the academy. He practiced military drills and became known for his horsemanship and skill as a military tactician.

Following his graduation on July 1, 1831, Second Lieutenant Emory was assigned to the 4th Artillery. As part of that unit, he served at Forts McHenry and Severn in Maryland, and at Charleston Harbor, South Carolina. Later he drew duty at Forts Hamilton and Lafayette in New York, and in 1836, he participated in the removal of the Creek Nation from Georgia to the Indian Territory.

Bored with garrison duty, on September 30, 1836, Emory resigned his commission after receiving an invitation from the Secretary of War to become an assistant United States civil engineer. This move made him eligible for an appointment to the Army Corps of Topographical Engineers. He liked this work and served in this capacity until July 7, 1838, when he achieved the rank of first lieutenant in the newly created Corps of Topographical Engineers.

Earlier explorations of the West by Lewis and Clark, Zebulon Pike, and William Hunter and John Dunbar had demonstrated the need for a professional corps of explorers and topographers. Pike made errors in his report because of inadequate scientific training; his estimate of the height of Pike's Peak was off by 4,000 feet, while a nearby latitude was wrong by some 35 miles. As a result, the Army began naming topographical officers to the service.

Topographical officers served as surveyors, explorers, and cartographers, and worked on federal civil engineering projects such as rivers and harbors. They did not compete with the officers in the Corps of Engineers, whose duties were narrowed to overseeing the construction and maintenance of military works such as coastal fortifications. In 1818, the War Department created a separate unit known as the Topographical Bureau under Major Isaac Roberdeau. It consisted of six men, who, as part of the Engineering Department, were to collect maps and reports of topographical projects.

In the aftermath of the War of 1812, Henry Clay called for internal improvements at federal expense—a network of roads, canals, and railroads—which necessitated a tremendous amount of topographical work. Congress gave its blessing in 1824 by passing the General Survey Act. In the ensuing years, the Army's topographical branch underwent organizational changes at the urging of Colonel John J. Abert, a graduate of West Point who was named Chief of the Bureau when Roberdeau died in 1829.

Abert argued that the differences between the two kinds of engineers in the Army—those concerned with topographical work and those who oversaw the construction of fortifications—justified two separate organizations. In 1831, Abert persuaded Congress to remove his topographers from the Engineering Department and place his bureau directly under the Secretary of War. After seven years of continued lobbying, he was named chief of an independent Corps of Topographical Engineers. For the Corps of Topographical Engineers, Abert recruited the best soldier-scientists in the Army, including William H. Emory.

That same year, 1838, prior to rejoining the Army, Emory in May married Matilda Wilkins Bache, a great granddaughter of Benjamin Franklin whose family was equal in social status to that of the Emorys. Matilda, a loving and devoted partner for the frequently absent army officer, gave birth to ten children. Emory's marriage brought him into a wealthy and politically powerful family. Matilda's father Alexander D. Bache was a director of the Coast and Geodetic Survey, and her brother-in-law Robert J. Walker was a leading member of the Democratic Party in Washington. Both men were close associates of George M. Dallas, vice-president under James K. Polk and a leading proponent of westward expansion.

Emory found joy in his marriage and his work with the Corps of Topographical Engineers. Abert directed a series of explorations that were undertaken by the Corps from 1838 to 1863. Sixty-four of the officers he appointed were West Point graduates who had been specially trained in a curriculum aimed at producing engineer-soldiers. From 1839 to 1842, Emory became an expert on harbor improvements. A year later, he was promoted to the post of assistant in the Topographical Bureau in Washington and then as principal assistant to Major James Duncan Graham, who had been given the enormously difficult job of surveying the boundary between the United States and Canada.

Emory's appointments brought out envy on the part of a few of his fellow officers in the Topographical Engineers. John M. Goldsborough charged that Emory's family used its influence to get him these prestigious appointments, whereupon Emory challenged him to a duel. He traveled to Baltimore with his brother Robert and his second, Major William Graham, prepared to defend his

William J. Emory of the Army Corps of Topographers surveyed the border from San Diego to the Rio Grande and set down Monument 26, which later became Monument 122 in the heart of Nogales. (Courtesy Library of Congress.)

honor with bullets. Fortunately, a few days before he arrived, Goldsborough was arrested for misconduct, and the duel was averted.

Emory's work on the Canadian boundary survey from 1844 to 1846 brought commendations for his surveying techniques from the British commissioners, who appreciated the skillful and physically demanding survey, which he completed during the severe winter months on the mountain ridges. In addition to his outstanding field work, Emory produced a superb map of the Republic of Texas, noting that his sources were filled with inaccuracies and stating that he was bound to repeat some errors because he had never actually seen the region. Both Emory and his commander, Colonel Abert, correctly suspected that many falsehoods were in the literature and maps of the Southwest. They believed it was imperative that verifiable data be compiled, assimilated, and published by the Corps. Thus, when the Army of the West was to be sent from Kansas to New Mexico and then on to California, Abert chose Emory, whom he believed best qualified by physical attributes, scholarship, and attitude, to accompany this expedition. In 1854, Major Emory and his Mexican counterpart José Salazar y Larregui, set out to mark the international boundary from San Diego to the Rio Grande in Texas.

Emory, always a hard task master, in May of 1855 sent an express rider to find out why his assistant Lieutenant Nathaniel Michler of the Corps of Topographical Engineers had not arrived in Santa Cruz. Michler sent back a sharp retort that it should have been obvious to Emory, who knew the country, why it took so long. Emory chose not to reprimand the exhausted young officer and waited. During this wait, he explored southern Arizona. He visited with John Pinkston in Tucson, who spoke of the presence of gold, silver, and copper, but warned against stories of rich treasures. Emory became more impatient with both Michler and the Mexicans. From his headquarters in Nogales, Mexico, he wrote: "I am . . . both from personal and official considerations, anxious to close this work and return home and would be very glad to see the Mexican government compelled to put its commission on a footing to aid me in so doing." He now considered court-martialing his young assistant, but later accepted the fact that Michler had put forth his best effort. While at Nogales, Arizona, Emory hosted a number of important visitors including a delegation of Indian chiefs led by Antonio Azul. They had traveled almost 200 miles and wished to discuss a new treaty signed on June 29, 1855. Emory assured Azul that the United States would abide by the treaties.

Today, a steel four-sided shaft stands just a few feet west of Morley in Nogales. Visitors, good and bad, and merchandise, legal and contraband, flow around it. On occasion, bullets have whizzed by the marker. When Emory left the Boundary Commission headquarters in Los Nogales Pass in 1855, he left behind a pyramid

Monument 26, which later became Monument 122, is the Gadsden Purchase boundary marker erected in 1855 by William H. Emory. (Sketch by J. Ross Browne.)

Antonio Azul led a delegation of Native American chiefs to meet with William H. Emory to discuss a new treaty. Azul was assured that the United States would uphold its end of the treaty. (Courtesy Arizona Historical Society.)

of stones marked "26," which established the site for a future and permanent Monument 122.

In November 1891, the Boundary Commission ordered Colonel J.W. Barlow of the Corps of Engineers to resurvey the boundary west of the Rio Grande. Barlow and Mexican engineer Jacobo Blanco stayed in Nogales from November 18, 1892 to January 11, 1893. Barlow described Monument 26 as a rude pile of stones occupying the middle point of the settlement and it was replaced with another monument. As Nogales began to develop into a town, the Brickwood Saloon covered about half of the monument; the sidewalk and the street were on Mexican soil.

3. Early Mining in Santa Cruz County

On February 22, 1879, a 20-year-old Frenchman, Alphonse Louis Pinart, sketched what remained of the Real de Arizonac. The Real de Arizonac, about 25 miles south of the present United States–Mexico border, provided Arizona with its name. This property was initially owned by Gabriel Prudhon de Bútrom y Mújica, the mayor of Sonora. When the Yaqui prospector Antonio Sirumea made a fabulous silver strike in 1736 here, swarms of prospectors took large silver balls (*bolas de plata)* and slabs (*planchas de plata)* and the area became known as the Real de Arizonac. Sirumea sold his interest for approximately 16 pesos. One boulder of silver, reported to weigh over a ton, had to be broken into pieces so it could be transported on burros.

An argument arose as to whether the discovery was a treasure cache, in which case it would belong entirely to the king of Spain, or whether it was a mine from which the king would derive a *quinto*, or 20 percent of the profits. Captain Juan Bautista de Anza, Sonora's chief justice, sought a legal decision, but decreed an embargo on the shipment of silver. The lawyers argued and it took several years before the courts determined that the silver bonanza came from a treasure trove. The captain's son, Juan Bautista de Anza II, a graduate of the College of Royal Engineers in Mexico City, served as commander of the Tubac Presidio and, in 1774, led an overland expedition from Tubac to California and founded San Francisco. He is buried in the church at Arizpe, Sonora.

One of the last to mine in the Real de Arizonac area was Karl Edward Höller. The family later dropped the umlaut from their name. Holler, born in Solingen, Prussia on September 8, 1841, graduated with an engineering degree from the University at Heidleberg after he completed his military service. Fluent in German, Swedish, French, Spanish, English, Russian, and Italian, he was offered a faculty chair in languages at Stanford University, but wanted to work in mining. His work took him to New York, Argentina, and Mexico. From Mexico he moved to Stanton, Iowa, where he married Sigrud Pierson, a native of Sweden. After their first child Edward was born in 1873, the family moved to San Francisco in a covered wagon. They moved to Tucson in 1879 and arrived in Nogales a year later. From there, they moved to Hermosillo, Mexico, where Karl engaged in various mining activities, including the Real de Arizonac. When a yellow fever epidemic raged in Mexico, the family returned to Nogales, where they found a less severe yellow fever epidemic. Holler continued his mining work along the border until he was killed when lightning struck a pole, which then landed on him, on August 3, 1903.

Several of Arizona's oldest mines are located in Santa Cruz County near Nogales, which was so proud of its mines that it built a smelter in the 1890s. The Spanish worked the Salero (salt cellar) Mine in the Santa Rita Mountains in the 1600s, which was worked in 1828 by the Mexicans, and by John and William Wrightson from Ohio in 1857. They and their associates H.C. Grosvenor and Gilbert W. Hopkins were killed by Apaches.

Even before southern Arizona became a part of the United States, Charles Debrille Poston saw its potential for mineral wealth. Poston, born in Hardin County, Kentucky on June 24, 1825, was orphaned at age 12. He apprenticed to the Hardin County Clerk's office where he studied law under Samuel Haycraft for seven years and married Haycraft's daughter Margaret in Elizabethtown, Kentucky. They had a daughter, Sarah Lee, and a second child who died shortly after birth. Margaret suffered several strokes before her death from cancer in 1884. After an apprenticeship with the Tennessee Supreme Court, Poston was admitted to the bar at age 22, and practiced in Tennessee and Washington, D.C. Lured by gold fever in 1850, Poston moved to San Francisco where he found work as a clerk

This sketch by Alphonse Pinart depicts the Real de Arizonac, the area 25 miles south of the current border between the United States and Mexico. The Real de Arizonac gave Arizona its name and Spain a treasure trove of silver. (Courtesy Bancroft Library.)

Karl Höller (in the black hat) was one of the last people to mine the Real de Arizonac. This photo from the late 1800s also shows his son Edward (the blonde boy in the front row). (Courtesy Pimería Alta Historical Society.)

in the customs house. Here he became friends with Mexico's powerful Iturbide family, whose contacts enabled him to become an agent for companies investing in Sonora, which included Tubac and Nogales.

When present-day southern Arizona became part of the United States in 1853, Poston led an exploration party, financed by French bankers, along the Gulf of California and into Arizona to seek out harbors and mineral deposits in these newly acquired lands. After completion of the exploration, Poston traveled to New York, where with backing from the Texas Pacific railroad, he organized the Sonora Exploring and Mining Company with Samuel Peter Heintzelman as president and Poston as general manager. He also secured a loan to purchase modern mining machinery and mining property.

In 1856, Poston and his armed party rode into the small Mexican village of Tucson. After acquiring provisions, they rode on to Tubac to take over the Spanish mines at Cerro Colorado and Arivaca. He purchased the Aribac ranch from Tomás and Ignacio Ortiz, who had acquired the property as a land grant in 1832. After setting up headquarters at Tubac, the company discovered several rich silver mines and employed more than 250 men. However, they were forced to flee when Apaches attacked Cerro Colorado and killed Poston's brother Lee. Lee Poston's lonely grave and tombstone are still near the mine.

As the unofficial mayor of Tubac, Poston performed marriages that the visiting priest, Father Joseph Machebeuf, declared illegitimate until Poston paid him $700. Poston issued paper money with pictures of animals so the village's illiterate population could visually determine the denominations of the notes. A chicken was worth 25¢, while a lion was worth $10. Poston described Tubac as a place whose only occupation was labor and whose only law was love. Today, Tubac boasts a plethora of art galleries featuring famous western artists, such as Hal Empie and Ross Stefan, and actively works to preserve its heritage.

Poston served as secretary to the Tucson Convention, which formulated procedures to secure local territorial government. A strong advocate of local government, he wrote, "Arizona has been a tarrying post for every passing political tramp for many years." Territorial government was put on hold with the onset of the Civil War and subsequent depredations by Apaches. Poston abandoned his Arizona mining enterprises and joined the Union forces. After the war, he lobbied in Washington, D.C. to create the Arizona Territory. When Arizona achieved territorial status, Poston had a silver ink stand created by Tiffany from Arizona silver as a gift to President Abraham Lincoln. The Lincoln family presented the inkstand to the Library of Congress.

In 1864, Poston became Arizona's first congressional delegate. He secured the first congressional appropriation for irrigation and advocated building irrigation works to aid reservation tribes to become self-supporting. He was defeated for reelection by a former Arizona governor, John Noble Goodwin.

This Santa Rita Copper Mining and Smelting Company stock certificate dates from 1905. Nogales was so proud of its mines that it built a smelter in the 1890s. (Courtesy Fred Holabird Americana.)

During his later years, Poston traveled and published a travel book, *Europe in the Summer-Time*, and worked as a foreign correspondent for the *New York Tribune*. He returned to Arizona to work as a register of the U.S. Land Office at Florence, and to write a book of poetry entitled *Apache Land*. For a man with only five years of formal education, Poston held several key government positions. He worked as consular clerk at Nogales; consular clerk, El Paso; clerk in the Department of Agriculture in Washington, D.C.; statistical clerk in the Department of Agriculture in Phoenix; and superintendent of the Agricultural Experimental Station in Phoenix. He helped form the Arizona Historical Society, but bitterly fought with the leadership over membership requirements and stomped out of a meeting, never to return.

In 1885, Poston married Martha Tucker, many years his junior and a former newspaper typesetter, in Flagstaff, but soon afterwards the couple separated, probably because Poston drank heavily. His son-in-law died in Manilla after the Spanish-American War and his daughter Sarah Lee died at sea on her voyage home from Manilla. The Arizona Territorial Legislature voted to give Poston a pension

The 16th Territorial Legislature in 1891 named Charles D. Poston (standing) the "Father of Arizona." Here he poses with Louis H. Chalmers of the House of Representatives, Maricopa County, and James H. Tevis of the House of Representatives, Cochise County. (Courtesy Arizona Historical Society.)

of $25 a month and named Charles Debrille Poston as the "Father of Arizona." On June 24, 1902, Poston died a pauper in Phoenix. In 1925, his remains were reinterred at the top of Poston's Butte near Florence where he had hoped to erect a temple to the Sun.

Only the Mowry Mine remained open when U.S. troops were transferred to fight in the Civil War. The well-fortified mine produced enough silver and gold to pay for the extraction of lead that Sylvester Mowry intended to sell to the Confederacy. Sylvester Mowry, a native of Providence, Rhode Island, was a descendant of Roger Mowry, who came to America in 1631. After graduation from West Point in 1852, Mowry was sent to Utah where the handsome young officer incurred Mormon wrath by showing an unseemly interest in their women. The military then transferred him to Fort Yuma, where he wrote, "Yuma is a hell of a place. More than two hundred miles from anywhere; in the midst of an Indian country . . ."

At Fort Yuma, Mowry, impressed with Arizona's mineral wealth, championed territorial organization. Never hampered by modesty, he identified himself so thoroughly with Arizona that at times it seemed as if he were the only one working for territorial status. In April 1860, Mowry purchased the Patagonia mine, which he renamed the Mowry, in southern Arizona. At age 28, he listed his occupation as "Retired U.S.A. Officer" in the 1860 census.

Mowry's activities formed the basis for allegations in the *New York Daily Tribune* that he and Samuel J. Jones of Mesilla were holding meetings all over the Territory to promote the Confederate cause. An unsigned letter from Tucson, dated March 20, appeared in the paper:

> The Secessionist movement has extended its baleful influence to this section of the Union . . . A fit instrument to aid the conspirators, Cobb, Floyd, Davis, Slidell, Toombs & Co., was found in Sylvester Mowry, the patriotic silver mine speculator and Squatter-Sovreignty bogus would be delegate to Congress from this Territory.

In the spring of 1861, Mowry and a party traveled to Guaymas, Mexico, where they sought support to have northern Mexico annexed to the United States, with Guaymas developed as an Arizona port. By July, he was back at the Mowry mine, where he started an extensive construction program to convert the property into a fortress, ostensibly against Apache depredations.

In the summer of 1861, Confederate troops under John R. Baylor invaded the Rio Grande Valley. At Mesilla, New Mexico, on August 1, Baylor issued a proclamation, taking possession of Arizona for the Confederate States and pronounced himself as military governor. General Henry H. Sibley arrived with a large Confederate force. Early in 1862, Sibley sent Captain Sherod Hunter's ranger company into Arizona, and Colonel James Reily traveled via Tucson to Hermosillo to set up a conference with Sonoran Governor Ygnacio Pesqueira. At the same time, General James Carleton, while preparing to move his California

Column, reported Confederate movements to his superior, General George Wright, commander of the Department of the Pacific. Reily's rank led Carleton to speculate that Sibley might cross Arizona in an attempt to invade California.

When Carleton reached Tucson on June 7, 1862, he established firm security during the afternoon. Captain Emil Fritz and his cavalry surrounded the town, arresting men with questionable loyalty to the Union cause. A Board of Officers investigated the personal and political status of these suspects. Several men took the Union oath of allegiance to secure their release, but others were removed to Fort Yuma for "safekeeping."

Carleton received a letter from T.L.R. Scheuner, a former Mowry mine employee, accusing Mowry of furnishing ammunition to a detachment from Sherod Hunter's company. He warned Carleton that Mowry was raising a six-pounder brass "to receive Northerners," and cautioned him not to try to take Mowry in the daytime because he had two men on the hill looking out for invaders. On June 8, Carleton ordered Lieutenant Colonel Edward E. Eyre to take 60 cavalry troopers commanded by Captain Fritz, and 25 infantrymen under Captain Edward B. Willis to arrest Mowry. Eyre's instructions read:

> You will seize all his personal papers and any documents of a political character that you may find on the premises, and bring them to this Head Quarters. You will also take into custody, and bring as prisoners to this post, all persons whom you find at the Patagonia Mines, using such discretion in your control of them as will prevent their doing anything to the prejudice of your movements, or to the U.S. Government.

Mowry reported that "General Carleton sent a Lieut. Colonel and one hundred and twenty-eight men to arrest me." Eyre reported that, at 1:00 a.m. on June 13, he left camp and marched to within 400 yards of Mowry's residence. Here he detached Captain Fritz and 30 men, with orders to surround and search each house and arrest all persons he might find there. Eyre, with the rest of the command, surrounded the corral, inside of which was Mowry's house.

At about 3:00 a.m., he knocked on the gate, which was at once opened by the night watchman. When Eyre asked the watchman if Lieutenant Mowry was at home, the watchman pointed to his bedroom door. Eyre knocked and Mowry appeared in his nightclothes. Eyre placed Mowry under arrest along with his workers. Mowry immediately asked for parole for himself and the others. Eyre declined.

Captain Willis and the infantry detachment remained at the mine to guard the property, while Eyre took his prisoners into headquarters at Tucson on June 16. A newspaper reported, "Mowry takes things quit coolly, puts on a good many airs, had along his mistress, Private Secretary, and servant. I think a dose of military treatment will cure him."

Carleton appointed a Board of Officers consisting of Colonel Joseph R. West, Captain Charles A. Smith, and Captain Nicholas Davis to determine

Sylvester Mowry purchased the Patagonia mine and renamed it after himself. He was accused of promoting the Confederate cause and convicted of treason. (Courtesy California State Library.)

whether the evidence justified holding Mowry for a formal accusation. The testimony concerned his pro-Confederate remarks wherein he admitted to giving ammunition to a detachment from Hunter's company, but claimed it was donated for fighting Apaches. The most damaging evidence came from his letters, which included his correspondence to Baylor, Jefferson Davis, Sibley, and Sherod Hunter.

In one letter dated October 24, 1861, addressed to Baylor, Mowry called attention to the "absolute necessity of making a display of the Confederate forces in this section of Arizona at the earliest possible moment." Disillusioned with his fellow Confederates, Mowry wrote Jefferson Davis:

> I think it is my duty to inform you that Col. Baylor seems to have fallen into the hands or to have gathered around him, a few irresponsible men utterly without character who may do the Territory and good cause infinite harm . . . The agent he has appointed to receive confiscated property [Palatine Robinson] is a man utterly dishonest, cowardly, and irresponsible, and I have known him for three years.

In a letter to Sibley, Mowry wrote that Arizona needed an efficient Apache extermination campaign and a strong military government until the Confederate

States of America could provide a civil government. He gave news of Union troop movements, which branded him as a traitor. After considering the evidence, the Board of Officers decided that there was "sufficient grounds to restrain the said Sylvester Mowry of his liberty and bring him to trial before a military Commission."

An undaunted Mowry requested a parole, claiming that he had unique mining expertise and powerful friends. Nothing swayed Carleton, who considered Mowry a traitor and a dishonorable man whose word could not be trusted. He described Mowry's residence as a place where blatant rebels could come and curse the government with impunity and without rebuke. Here gathered men who "having the reputation of being ruffians, as well as rebels, could come for shelter and food. In open and undisguised rebellion, they obtained ammunition with which to attack the troops of the Republic."

Carleton directed that Mowry be sent to Fort Yuma where he would remain in custody until otherwise ordered by competent authority. Under armed guard, Mowry traveled from Tucson to Fort Yuma on July 4, 1862. General Wright convened a Board of Officers in San Francisco to examine the evidence against Mowry and the others. Because Mowry's offense was committed in what was then New Mexico Territory, the Board held that he should be tried in the federal courts of that territory. Wright agreed and ordered Carleton to arrange for Mowry's trial in Santa Fe.

On October 12, 1862, Chief Justice Kirby Benedict of New Mexico wrote Carleton that, after reading the documents, the evidence created a deep impression of the "treasonable complicity of Mowry with the rebels." Benedict concluded that the government could not overlook his acts, and that Third Judicial Court at Albuquerque was the proper seat of jurisdiction. However, the judge also considered the practical obstacles of bringing Mowry to trial. Because the roads were unsafe, it would be necessary for a United States Marshal with an escort to travel to Yuma and return with the prisoner. Most of the witnesses were in Tucson and would also have to travel a considerable distance. Benedict concluded that there was "not a sufficient jail," in Albuquerque and hoped that another solution might be found.

As the theater of the war moved out of the Southwest where the Confederate cause had been rendered harmless, there was less interest in prosecuting Mowry. By the end of the summer, there was a move to extend amnesty to Arizona secessionists. A letter from the Judge Advocate's office in Washington directed the commander of Fort Yuma to determine whether the prisoner should be held or set free. The Board ordered his release on November 4, 1862. Of Mowry, Carleton wrote, "I have no feelings toward this man except such as arise from the conviction that he is a traitor and a spy."

Mowry continued to insist that he had not helped the Confederates, but that he had asked both factions for protection from the Apaches. He accused Carleton of illegal confiscation of his mine and sued him in the California courts for more than $1 million. In 1868, the government paid him $40,000. After the Civil

War, Mowry returned to Arizona once more and attempted to run for territorial delegate, but found no support in the territory. The *Tucson Citizen* wrote, "He quit the Territory having sustained his position as an egoist, braggart, and shameless liar." Mowry became seriously ill in 1871 and traveled to London to consult a specialist. On October 17, just four months short of his 39th birthday, Sylvester Mowry died of Bright's disease in a London hotel.

With peace and renewed investments, new mines were discovered and ones such as the Trench and Salero were relocated in the Santa Rita and Patagonia Mountains, and the Ostrich and the Yellow Jacket gold mines relocated north of Oro Blanco in 1876. The Hermosa silver mine in the Patagonia Mountains within two years produced about $1 million in silver bullion.

In the Oro Blanco Mountains west of Nogales, the Montana Ledge at Ruby was discovered in 1880 when a shady promoter styling himself as the Honorable H.J. Luttrell purchased the Holland Smelting and Mining Company for $60,000. The company failed largely because of mismanagement of funds. When the demonetization of silver in 1893 devastated Santa Cruz County's mines, attention turned to gold. New mills were built at the Montana, Austerlitz, Yellow Jacket, and Old Glory gold mines.

Ultimately, the electrification of homes and the copper industry saved the mining industry in the 1890s. The Pride of the West in the Patagonia Mountains and the Duquesne Mining and Reduction Company were financed by the Westinghouse Electrical Company. From 1912 through 1920, the Duquesne Mining and Reduction Company produced $6.5 million in copper, lead, zinc, silver, and gold. The major copper producer, the Three R Mine, was owned by rancher and miner Rollin Rice Richardson, who founded the town of Patagonia. After a series of litigation, the mine went into receivership, but during its years of production, the Three R Mine produced 85 million pounds of copper and 900,000 ounces of silver. The World's Fair Mine in the Patagonia Mountains, developed entirely without outside initial capital by Frank and Josephine Powers, provided the Powers family with enough small rich shipments to earn them a comfortable living. It was placed in receivership in 1927 and then bonded to the Zero Mining Company, which also acquired the neighboring Trench and Josephine mines. From 1900 through 1929, the World's Fair Mine brought in about $550,000 in silver, copper, and lead.

In 1877, a group of New York financiers formed the Hermosa Mining Company at Harshaw. Its mill, while in operation, was the largest in Arizona and its production of silver in 1880 was valued at $365,654.49. In 1877, James Finley of Tucson purchased the mine and reopened it in 1890. Another silver price drop devastated Harshaw and it became a ghost town.

The Trench Mine, first located prior to the Civil War by Colonel H.T. Titus, had been abandoned in 1861. Development resumed in the 1880s when it was leased by Hagan and Tevis, but a drop in the silver price made operations unprofitable and all work ceased in 1894. The mine reopened in 1912 when it was bonded to Senator Clark of Montana, who operated it under the name of the Trench Consolidated Mines Company with good production of silver and lead. Other mining properties in Santa Cruz County included the Alto; the Baca Float Mines; the Wandering Jew Mine, so named by Mark Lulley, an early Jewish pioneer; the Josiah Bond Mines; the Temporal Gulch Mines; the Mansfield Mines; and the Old Glory.

Oro Blanco, named for its white gold, became such a money maker that, in 1874, the Prefect of Altar and Governor Anion P.K. Safford of Arizona had this portion of the border resurveyed to make certain it was inside the United States borders. Dr. Adolphus H. Noon, the Oro Blanco correspondent for the *Chicago Tribune,* wrote, "A boom is working up here, many locations assaying high in gold and silver." Mineral ore was shipped to the port of Guaymas, Sonora, and then to such faraway places as Swansea in Wales. Mule-drawn wagons and wooden wheeled carretas pulled by yoked oxen transported nails, flour, and other commodities.

Adolphus Noon, born in London, had served with the British Cavalry in South Africa before coming to the United States. Although he wanted to work the mines, his services as a doctor were needed in Nogales. For many years, he was the only doctor between Tucson and Hermosillo. Noon often took cattle in lieu of cash from his patients. However, in 1889, he lost all of his cattle to the drought and had to start over again. Besides serving as a doctor, Noon also became mayor of Nogales.

Roy & Titcomb, one of the earliest Nogales businesses, supplied the mines with heavy machinery. Edward Titcomb and Colonel Bill Roy's business expanded into

Edward Titcomb formed a partnership with Colonel Bill Roy and established one of the earliest Nogales businesses to supply mines in Arizona and Mexico with heavy machinery.

a foundry and lumber mills. They made a fortune, but lost it during the Great Depression. Titcomb, born in Windham, New Hampshire to shipping merchant Edward Sr. and Sarah Abbot Titcomb, attended public schools before traveling west and engaging in silver mining in Colorado, New Mexico, and Arizona. After settling first in Nogales, they went on to Mexico where Titcomb worked five years in Sonora. In 1889, he formed a partnership with Colonel Roy that became Roy & Titcomb. He also served as an organizer of the First National Bank of Nogales, a director of the Nogales Electric Light, Ice and Water Company, and the Arizona and Sonora Manufacturing Company. Titcomb and his wife, the former Mary G. Christ of Nogales, were the parents of six children.

H.M. Clagett, vice president of Roy & Titcomb, was instrumental in the development of the Pride of the West. Clagett, born in Maryland on December 30, 1870, received his public school and mining engineering education in Maryland. In 1891, he traveled to Durango, Mexico, where for ten years he worked at copper mining. In 1902, he became superintendent of the Pride of the West. He championed the Arizona-Sonora Manufacturing Company and served as a director of the First National Bank of Nogales. Clagett also owned 60 thoroughbred Jersey cattle, which took first prize for three years at the Arizona State Fair. Clagett married Cora Rathbun, also a native of Maryland. He helped his wife organize the Ladies' Auxiliary of Santa Cruz Club.

Today, only the voices of ghosts whisper of the past glory of mining at places such as Harshaw and the Mowry. Except for a brief resurgence during World War II, the Santa Cruz County mines are but reminders of a time past.

H.M. Clagett not only developed the Pride of the West near Nogales, but he also assisted his wife, Cora Rathbun, with organizing the Ladies' Auxiliary of Santa Cruz Club.

4. EARLY RANCHING IN SANTA CRUZ COUNTY

Southern Arizona ranchers lived a solitary life, making them convenient prey for thieves and murderers. In 1857, Elias Green Pennington, with his 12 motherless children, established a ranch near the United States–Mexico border. The Pennington stone house has been preserved by Cabot Sedgwick. Originally from South Carolina, the Pennington family had wandered since 1832 through Tennessee, Missouri, and Texas. Elias intended to move to California, but he stopped along the Santa Cruz River and set a ranch. After the Apaches captured his daughter Larcena, they tossed her over a cliff in the Santa Rita Mountains. She survived the fall, landed on a snow bank, and for 16 days subsisted on roots and grass. Larcena Pennington lived to a very old age and saw her husband, father, and two brothers killed by Apaches.

Francisco Padrés, a Magdalena merchant who supplied the mines and the military with vegetables and flour, owned a pack train. On June 27, 1857, his 45-mule pack train slowly plodded past the Pennington ranch after making a delivery to Fort Buchanan. Five tough-looking men who had been following the train hid near the border in a grove of black walnut trees. Two of the men, known only as Davis and Ward, had come from California. When the Padrés party moved south across the border, the outlaws caught up with them and shot and killed several of the packers. They took off with the mules and herded the booty back toward Tucson. When the local settlers discovered their hideout, they informed Major Enoch Steen at Fort Buchanan, then joined the soldiers in arresting Davis and Ward. The citizens' posse jailed Ward at Fort Buchanan and returned most of the stolen property to Padrés. Because no authorized law enforcement existed within several miles, Steen released Ward. The settlers, outraged that murderers and robbers had been turned loose upon the community, started to establish a vigilante committee, but cooler heads prevailed. The settlers petitioned Congress to establish civil authority and averted the unhappy prospect of lynching.

While Larcena convalesced from mountain fever, her father decided to move to California. But he decided to stay when he secured a contract from the Fort Buchanan quartermaster to furnish hay for the army horses. Elias and his sons cut

Pete Kitchen, a famous Santa Cruz County rancher, kept both hogs and cattle. After American troops left to fight in the Civil War, Kitchen remained and protected his home.

the tall wild grass on the hillsides, loaded it on ox-drawn wagons and hauled it to the fort. To his great disappointment, the quartermaster had run out of money and Pennington did not receive any pay that summer.

Pete Kitchen, one of the most famous ranchers in southern Arizona, added hogs to his ranch, along with his large cattle herd. Kitchen became famous for humor and his hams graced many a table from Nogales to Santa Fe. Peter Kitchen, born in Covington, Kentucky in 1822, joined the Army in 1846 and served along the Rio Grande for two years with the Mounted Rifles Regiment. After he was mustered out in Oregon, the gold rush beckoned him, but he appears to have had no success as a prospector. He arrived in Tucson just before the signing of the Gadsden Purchase in 1853.

Kitchen saw the 1856 mining boom and the opening of several mines in the Santa Rita and Cerro Colorado Mountains. However, ranching appealed to him and he ranched at La Canoa north of Tubac before founding El Potrero, "the pasture" on the fertile fields along Potrero Creek less than 5 miles from the United States–Mexico border near Kino's Guevavi Mission. He fortified his house with thick adobe walls and was the only rancher to stay in the area after American troops left to fight in the Civil War. Kitchen, always wary of Apache attacks, could still joke about the danger. He called the road "Tucson, Tubac, Tumacácori and

Tohell." When General Crook and a party of soldiers visited Kitchen's ranch in 1870, Kitchen's sentinel paced the parapet on the roof, another guard stood watch with the stock, and the men plowing the fields carried rifles, cocked and loaded, swinging from the plow handle. Kitchen, who waged a continual war with the Apaches, described his pigs filled with arrows, making the suffering quadrupeds look like perambulating Apache pincushions.

Kitchen hired Francisco Verdugo and married his sister, Rosa. He also hired Manuel Ronquillo, who had married Verdugo's other sister Jesús, and the three families ran the El Potrero ranch. Both Ronquillo and Verdugo were trustworthy and intelligent and expert horsemen. Most important, all three men were crack rifle and pistol shots. Kitchen's home became a haven for travelers, who never went away hungry. His wife Rosa, along with her five nieces and servants, took care of the domestic duties and the ranch had its own blacksmith, saddle, and wagon maker.

In 1871, Kitchen's adopted 12-year-old son Santiago was killed by Apaches after he fell asleep in the haystack. The cemetery at El Potrero contained the graves of his wife's family and many workers. Frontier life never left much time for grief.

Rosa Verdugo Kitchen, here in the middle of two of her nieces, Polonia Verdugo de Casanega and Nieves Verdugo de Arros, took care of the domestic duties on the ranch.

Manuel Ronquillo, Pete Kitchen's brother-in-law, married Francisco Verdugo's other sister, Jesús. Ronquillo and his family helped the Kitchens run the El Potrero ranch.

Kitchen made frequent trips to Tucson and one newspaper announced his arrival with the words "Peter Kitchen, whom not to know is to acknowledge one's self unknown." On one return to his ranch, he discovered that every head of stock was gone and he had to begin his ranching from scratch.

Military camps provided additional revenue for Kitchen. On August 21, 1865, Fort Mason was established near Calabasas. Camp Cameron was erected in the Santa Rita Mountains on October 1, 1866 and, two years later, work began on Camp Crittenden. Kitchen delivered fresh pork, cured hams, and sides of bacon to the quartermasters at these military establishments. He also supplied the military with lard, potatoes at 12¢ per pound, corn, and plenty of earthy frontier stories. Kitchen believed that "life was grim enough without pulling a long face and short enough, unless the gods were kind, to warrant getting a full measure of pleasure while it lasted."

Kitchen became good friends with Tucsonan Fred Maish, whose heavy German accent and speech blunders were a constant source of merriment. When Kitchen went into a Tucson hospital with spleen problems, a couple cowboys tiptoed into the sickroom and asked, "What's the matter with him?" Maish replied, "Doc

43

Handy says his screen's out of whack." The *Arizona Citizen* kept its readers up to date on the health of the popular Kitchen. On his recovery, the newspaper wrote:

> We believe a change of air for a short period is all that is needed to make him what he was—not a very fat man to be sure—but healthy and wiry and good for a long life. He is bringing a lot of bacon and potatoes and his ranch products are always the best.

In 1880, Kitchen sold his ranch for $60,000 and moved to Tucson with Rosa and her nieces. He loved drinking and gambling and before long all the money disappeared. What he did not lose at gambling, he lost on mining investments. When Kitchen died at age 77 on August 5, 1895, the Arizona Pioneers Historical Society paid $40 for his funeral.

Arthur L. Peck, whose interest in Santa Cruz County involved mining, ranching, and public service, was born in Chautauqua County, New York in March 1845. He left the Empire State for Minneapolis, Minnesota, and from there moved on to engage in mining at Virginia City and the gold mines of Bodie, California and Sonora, Mexico. In Sonora, he became connected with the Preatus Mining Company, controlling important gold ore properties and operating a 40-stamp mill. His ranching endeavor flourished in Peck's Canyon until his wife and child were killed during an Apache raid. After this disaster, Peck returned to Sonora, where he accepted the position of superintendent of El Promontorio Mine. He also established a Nogales livery business and acquired several valuable mining interests. His second marriage to Carmen Cainas produced four children. Peck gave "stalwart allegiance to the Republican party" and served on the Nogales City Council, Santa Cruz County board of supervisors, and as Nogales street commissioner. As street commissioner, Peck supervised the filling of a large arroyo at the end of Grand Avenue. Although Morley Street merchants bitterly opposed the project fearing they would lose business, it provided a third access road between Ambos Nogales.

During the drought in the summer of 1885, many ranchers were forced to sell off their cattle at a loss or the animals would face starvation. Then came the rains and the grass came back to normal. Two laws helped Arizona ranchers. All Arizona cattle ranchers were required to register their brands and all Sonoran cattle were declared to be diseased and quarantined at the border. Colin Cameron was the first to register his "6T" brand.

Colin Cameron founded the San Rafael Ranch in the late 1800s. Cameron, a native of Lancaster County, Pennsylvania, acquired land in Arizona in 1884. He incurred the wrath of several neighbors who formed the Settlers Protective Association, which destroyed several of his fences and may have burned his house down. They warned that if he took legal action they would "burn all your corrals and every ranch you own or pretend to own." Many felt that Cameron had simply appropriated land that belonged to others. The San Rafael Ranch was part of the old San Rafael de la Zanja Land Grant issued in 1825 by the Mexican

Arthur L. Peck stands in front of his Nogales livery stable. After his wife and child were killed in an Apache raid, Peck returned to Sonora. (Courtesy Pimería Alta Historical Society.)

government to Manuel Bustello. In 1909, Cameron sold the ranch to Colonel William C. Greene, a copper mining magnate in Cananea, Sonora. When Greene's daughter Florence Sharp inherited the property, it became home to the Greene Cattle Company.

Enter the ladies into Santa Cruz County ranching: Carrie Frazier and Rhoda McCarthy. Never had two more high-spirited women arrived on the Elgin community scene than Carrie Swigart and her sister Rhoda. Carrie had taught school for a while and both sisters attended the Pierce Business School in Philadelphia. They both had good jobs in lawyers' offices in Washington, D.C. in 1910, when they received a letter from their sister Esther Rothrock, who lived in Elgin, to come and homestead land. Esther's description of warm sunny Arizona was irresistible and on a cold muddy March day in 1913, they "burned their bridges" and set out for Arizona.

From Washington, they could only buy tickets to Benson, which the conductor said had only a water tank. He thought maybe there might be a train out of Benson that would take them to Elgin. Their train traveled 20 miles per hour and slowed down to 10 miles per hour over bridges. In Benson, they secured tickets to Elgin along with owners of poultry and various small livestock. Their brother-in-law Bruce Rothrock met them at Elgin with a lumber wagon. Along the way to their sister's house, they got their first glimpse of the majestic Mount Baldy. They knew Esther and her family were living in a one-room lean-to, so Carrie and Rhoda each brought their own cot and chair.

Colin Campbell founded the San Rafael Ranch in the late 1800s and offended many of his neighbors in the process. (Courtesy Pimería Alta Historical Society.)

By the time they arrived in Arizona, all the desirable homesteads had been picked, but they camped on the edge of the available property. The first night they were invited to dinner by one of the bachelor "squatters" who lived in a dugout. At the dugout entrance, his roof was covered with green oak poles that sagged when they dried out. Over the top of the poles was a layer of bear grass, and the front of the dugout had a door and a window. To keep out the rain, Jim Frazier had hung a large dishwater tub over his bed. Carrie said later, "I married this Gink." Rhoda married Jim McCarthy. Jim Frazier, Elgin's unofficial mayor, had a part as a trapper in the epic movie *Red River*. This movie, filmed near Elgin, told the story of the first cattle drive over the old Chisholm trail.

To take possession of their property, the Swigart sisters had to build a house on their land. Rhoda stayed on her land until she died 30 years later. Carrie moved onto her husband's land because he already had a well. Frazier and his two brothers had already harvested two good crops so they always had plenty to eat. After dinner, he drove Carrie and Rhoda in his buckboard pulled by a mule team to look over the best spots where the sisters could "prove up." They were in their early 30s and each had a few thousand dollars saved up. After two weeks of camping, at 4:00 p.m. on March 29, 1913, a man rode up and said that two families were leaving and the sisters could file on the abandoned property. At sundown, the sisters loaded up their trunks, bedding, a coffeepot, a skillet, a load of homemade bread, bacon and eggs, and their cots and chairs on Jim's wagon and made their move during night. They found where the previous families had staked their pegs and set up one cot on each side of the iron pegs. They furnished two tents—one for sleeping and the other for their cooking. Each sister claimed 260 acres. Over an early morning breakfast and a beautiful sunrise, they beheld their land.

Single women were a rarity and, before long, many young single bachelors were helping the Swigart sisters get settled. One man hauled wood and lent them an axe to cut it. Another contributed enough wire to keep wild cattle away. For a stove, the men took a 5-gallon kerosene can and cut one end out, drilling a hole in the other end to let the smoke out. The Frazier boys brought much-appreciated pails of fresh drinking water. After the men chopped wood, they usually stayed to help eat a meal of beef or a savory rabbit stew. During their first three years, there was plenty of rain and the grass grew tall around the tents and cooking areas. Then someone decided to burn off the grass and, no sooner than they did, a puff of wind came along and their bedding and tents burned up. The fire raged until it came to a place where horses had eaten the grass short and then it went out by itself.

Carrie and Rhoda were never disconsolate for long. One night, it rained hard and their tents leaked. They slept on one cot under the umbrella for the rest of the night. During the early days of their arrival, the sisters decided to climb a hill, but took no thought of bringing food or water. They reached the top of the hill and when they looked around, they realized that they were lost. Every hill looked alike. They split when Rhoda tried to find the way around a hill and Carrie went to go over it. Carrie found her way home several hours before Rhoda. Both were hungry and thirsty. On another excursion, they found a stove that had been left at a government surveyor's camp, which they carried home over 2.5 miles of rugged terrain.

Carrie and Jim Frazier's first house was a 12-foot-by-14-foot room with a floor and windows and a door that could be shut. The sisters learned to bake bread, which took some adjustment after moving from sea level to 5,000 feet elevation. After a house, Carrie acquired a small mustang mare and Rhoda bought a colt. The colt came with a little wagon and harness and Carrie bought a small saddle. When a friend brought them four empty kegs, they could haul the water instead of paying $1 per barrel for it. To do their laundry, they walked 6 miles to their sister Esther's home and stayed over night. The next morning, they walked a couple more miles to the Rothrock family home where they did the laundry with water pulled up from a 200-foot deep well. They washed their own clothes plus that of Esther's family, which included a baby. With their horses they could ride, but the little mare could be stubborn and hated to haul water or washing.

During the Mexican Revolution, fighting occurred only 20 miles from their homestead. When Carrie accidentally rode into the rebels' camp, the soldiers shouted when they saw a woman and Carrie later remarked that she never knew her horse could run that fast. One day, Carrie rode her mare into a pond to get a drink of water. The horse liked it so much that she waded into the middle of the pond and laid down in the water. Carrie stepped off as the horse went down and stood in water and mud up to her waist.

Carrie and Rhoda learned to make jelly from wild grapes and pies with manzanita berries. They discovered that the small native walnuts made delicious cookies and that careless weed could be used as a vegetable. During their second year, they planted beans and corn. To fulfill the homestead law, a neighbor A.C. Dalton plowed 5 acres of sod for them. They planted pink beans in double rows. Over the years, the Fraizers increased their holdings to 6,000 acres. Carrie gave up riding at 80, but until a few months before her death on Christmas Eve of 1973, 92-year-old Carrie Frazier was often seen driving her pickup truck and herding cattle on her ranch.

Carrie Swighart Frazier, a pioneering ranch woman in Santa Cruz County, continued herding cattle until she was 92. (Courtesy Pimería Historical Society.)

5. A Gathering at a Grove of Walnuts: 1850–1880

The U.S. Boundary Commission drew the "Line" between Mexico and the United States right through Los Nogales Pass. Today, tourists passing between Nogales, Arizona and Nogales, Mexico seldom notice the 6-foot Monument 122, which Fred and Harriet Rochlin described as the "heart of Ambos Nogales." Legal and illegal merchandise, criminals, and honest citizens flow by the monument and in the past, bullets and bombs flew by in total defiance of international treaties. High on a hill to the west stands the lonely Monument 121, marking another dividing spot.

When Major William H. Emory's party abandoned its headquarters at the Los Nogales Pass in October 1855, the surveyors left behind a pyramid of stones marked "26" that established the site for the present Monument 122. During the next several decades, Mexican and American merchants set up commercial ventures around the monument. Border merchants built their businesses as close to the line as possible to take advantage of tax-free trade, a practice discouraged by U.S. Customs officials.

Juan José Vásquez opened a roadhouse on the Sonora side and Jacob Isaacson built his one-room adobe store on the American side. Born in 1853 in Gulding, Russia (now Poland), the Isaacson family moved to London and then they, with Jakob and his elder brother Isaac, emigrated to New York. In 1880, Jacob and Isaac traveled to Tucson, Arizona, where they sold clothing and pots and pans. When they learned that a transcontinental railroad would be crossing Arizona, they correctly guessed that it would be in the Nogales area.

In 1880, Jacob set up a trading post in the grove of walnut trees in Nogales Pass where he lived alone. The community's first name was Isaacson and Jacob became Isaacson's first postmaster. Variations of Isaactown and Isaacville may be found in early history publications and maps. In 1883, the citizens voted to change the town name from Isaacson to Nogales. Jacob's store, which provided supplies and groceries to railroad workers, miners, ranchers, and the military, was listed in *McKenney's Pacific Coast Director for 1883–1884*. About a year later, he left for Mexico where he became very ill. After his recovery, he started a number of successful businesses in Oregon, California, Missouri, and Texas.

Jacob Isaacson founded Nogales and became its first postmaster. The town was originally named Isaacson. (Courtesy Abe Rochlin.)

After his first wife, Bessie Wolf, died in 1902, leaving him with four children, he married Jennie Pierce, a widow with a child in El Paso. When he returned from a business trip, he discovered that Jennie had taken all his possessions and deserted him. Jacob, in a deep depression, visited his sister in Detroit, where he recovered, but for the next two decades spent time in and out of mental institutions. Jacob returned several times to Arizona and visited Nogales in 1900, which by then had a population of 1,700. In a 1910 interview with the Douglas *Daily Dispatch*, he reminisced, with a faraway look in his eyes:

> It was lonely in those times, yes very lonely. On some days there would be little or no travel and during the nights I had only the stars to keep me company. On top of this solitude the Apaches were still in the land and always there existed the awful dread that they would come in the dead of night and with the rising of the sun, and find me unprepared to fight for my life. More than one visit did I get from them, but I always managed to get away with my life.

Jacob Isaacson died on December 27, 1928 in a mental institution, but the cause of death was listed as cerebral arteriosclerosis. Jacob lies buried in Section B,

Row 3 of the Machpelah Cemetery in Ferndale, Michigan. His burial site was discovered only after long hours of research by former Nogales Mayor Abe Rochlin. Abe's father Jake Rochlin arrived in the United States in 1917 and ultimately settled in Nogales, where he joined his brother-in-law J.B. Robinson in the scrap metal business.

John Brickwood is credited with being Nogales's first permanent resident. From his Exchange Saloon, which enveloped Monument 122, Brickwood, who also served two terms as mayor, sold cigars from a case attached to the Mexican side of his saloon, thereby avoiding import duties. From time to time, a fugitive would stop in the Exchange Saloon on the United States side, fortify himself with a glass of red-eye, and sneak out the back door into Mexico, confident that he was beyond the jurisdiction of an American court. When Brickwood's Exchange Saloon was razed in 1897, Monument 122 was allowed to stand free and, a year later, Congress removed from any use except as a public highway a 2-mile, 60-foot wide strip along the border. Other early border businesses included La Bonanza, The Casino, The Red House, and the International Bank of Nogales.

Jacob Isaacson's tombstone is in Michigan. This was put on his grave site in recent years thanks to the effort of former Nogales mayor Abe Rochlin and the Pimería Alta Historical Society.

La Moda, Franco Brothers Groceries, La Francas, and the Gem lined the border on the Sonora side.

On January 5, 1924, the 25th Infantry in full military dress marched in half step to a funeral dirge leading the citizens of Nogales to the cemetery to pay final respects to pioneer Anton Proto. From its inception as a town, the Proto brothers Anton and Louis were involved with Nogales. The Proto firm operated one of the largest mercantile concerns in Nogales and a magnificent ranch in Sonora. Anton and Louis, born in Macedonia, Greece, emigrated to America as young men in 1878. They brought with them sponges from their native land, which they sold at a profit in New York. From New York, they traveled to Panama where they worked as interpreters in several languages until they moved to San Francisco in 1879. Two years later, they settled in Tucson in 1881, where for a while they ran a restaurant. They then moved to Tombstone, where they established themselves as grocers. After their Tombstone business was destroyed by fire, they made and sold adobe brick and prospected in Sonora, Mexico.

In 1882, the brothers settled permanently in Nogales, where they continued their business ventures, including a bakery, until Louis died on March 7, 1909. The Proto ranch in Sonora covered a quarter of a million acres of land that provided pasture for several thousand high-bred Hereford cattle. The first Proto

John T. Brickwood, Nogales's first permanent settler, served two terms as mayor and owned the Exchange Saloon encircling Monument 122.

Anton Proto, Nogales's first elected mayor, emigrated to America from Greece along with his brother Louis. (Courtesy Pimería Alta Historical Society.)

mercantile on Morley Avenue was an 8- by 10-foot adobe room crowded with merchandise and sacks of flour, beans, and green coffee stacked to the ceiling. Anton developed the jobbing business with the help of his nephews Spiro, Anton, and Manuel. He served for four terms on the Nogales city council and was elected mayor in Nogales's first general election in 1894. In his will, Anton left cash donations to Nogales hospitals, schools, and fire department and to his native town of Beppora in Macedonia.

Edward Titcomb left his New Hampshire birthplace in 1877 at age 14 and explored Colorado and New Mexico for six years before coming to Nogales. Titcomb described the early Montezuma hotel as a board shack where gamblers and dance hall girls made such a ruckus in the early morning hours that he had to go out and walk the streets. Titcomb worked at several Mexico mines before permanently settling in Nogales in 1888 where he established a mining equipment sales business, the Arizona and Sonora Mining Company. He invited his friend Colonel William Roy to be his partner and do the book work. Before long, Titcomb discovered that Roy was unsuited to accounting, but that he was good with people. Roy and Titcomb also operated sugar, hardwood, and steel businesses and worked on the installation of the first telephone system in Hermosillo, Mexico.

Edward Titcomb and partner Colonel Billy Roy established a mining machinery firm, the Arizona and Sonora Mining Company in Nogales. (Courtesy Pimería Alta Historical Society.)

Their partnership continued until Roy's death in 1900, when Roy & Titcomb incorporated with Titcomb as president and Leander W. Mix, who bought Roy's interest, as vice president. H.M. Clagett and Louis Hudgin were board members. The Arizona and Sonora Mining Company had the best foundry and machine shops, and the largest stock of mining machinery in the Southwest. Titcomb also helped organize the First National Bank of Nogales and the Nogales Electric Light, Ice and Water Company. He died at the age of 93 in 1956. On February 1, 2002 Edward's grandson Reverend James Titcomb presented the Titcomb family history at a meeting of the Pimería Alta Historical Society.

Leopold Ephraim, born in Chulm, Prussia (now Poland) on April 16, 1850, left Europe for America in 1869 to avoid Russian military service. For a while, he worked in the south where he contracted malaria and was advised to seek a drier climate. In Montana, he purchased a wagon and a mule team and, with a load of clothing and household utensils, set out as a peddler. In 1877, he became a naturalized citizen and married Jenny Judah, who died soon after their marriage. Ephraim did well until a stock market crash put him out of business.

In San Francisco, devastated by bank failures, unemployment, drought, and anti-Chinese outbreaks, Ephraim suffered such a severe financial disaster that he walked most of the way from San Francisco to Tucson. He had heard about opportunities in mining at such places as Tombstone and the Silver King in Globe, Arizona. In Tucson, he found an old friend, Albert Steinfeld, who grubstaked him with merchandise and a stagecoach ride to Tubac where he opened the village's first store. Ephraim's Tubac store prospered, but he slept on a cot and arranged sacks of grain, flour, and sugar around his tent to deflect Apache arrows. In Nogales, he set up a tent store and, by all accounts, prospered. The Ephraim building was completed on his tent site at 114 Morley Avenue, just one block from the Unites States–Mexico border. Ephraim brought his father Gumpricht Ephraim to live with him. Gumpricht set up an assay shop, but in 1897, the old man fell ill and Ephraim took him to San Francisco where he died.

Ephraim continued to invest in Sonoran mining properties and he owned four claims near Tumacácori. At one time, his El Promontorio mine in Sonora produced so much silver that he employed a work force of 300 men, mostly Chinese. The *Tombstone Epitaph* described the road that Ephraim built to the mine as one of the best mountain roads in the Southwest. He donated enough acreage for a public cemetery in Ephraim Canyon northwest of the town.

Ephraim also provided Nogales with its first water company when he dug a large well and laid water lines to Nogales homes. When Nogales incorporated, the town wanted to buy his water company, but its coffers were so empty that no one would buy bonds to facilitate the sale. On February 12, 1912, two days before Arizona achieved statehood, the sale was consummated for $60,000 with the help of several wealthy investors.

In 1909, Ephraim, age 59, returned to Germany where he married his childhood sweetheart Franzisca Rosenthal. Upon their return to Nogales, they made their home on Crawford Street. His wife, however, developed respiratory

Leopold Ephraim and a worker pose at the Nogales Water Company. Ephraim suffered much financial hardship before prospering in Nogales. (Courtesy Abe Chanin.)

troubles and Dr. Adolphus H. Noon advised them to move to a lower altitude. They chose Los Angeles. His wife went ahead and waited for Leopold while he concluded his business in Arizona and Mexico. Ephraim put Ramon Vásquez, a friend and business associate, in charge of his Nogales holdings. When the Ephraims returned to Europe for a visit in 1914, they ran into trouble returning to the United States when World War I broke out. However, they made it home and lived out their days in California. Leopold Ephraim died on August 10, 1923 and is buried in Los Angeles, and his wife died in 1946. Nogales newspaperman Hanson R. Sisk wrote: "Leopold Ephraim was a man of fine character. He made business decisions with great caution. He was charitable, had a keen sense of humor and sympathized with those who were less fortunate because he himself had once drunk from the dregs of poverty."

Ramón Vásquez, Ephraim's friend, was born in Tucson in 1858 and attended the first Tucson public school in 1871. After completing his education, he went to work in Louis Zeckendorf's dry goods house and later opened his own store on Meyer Street. In 1885, he sold his interests in the Tucson store and moved to Nogales, where he established the Casa Colorado or the Red House. The Red House, a two-story structure of brick and stone with plate glass windows and the interior open to the ceiling, occupied a building on the east side of Morley Avenue near International Street. At the top of the stairway, the cashier's and packing departments connected to all parts of the store by automatic carriers. Besides his Nogales business and real estate investments, Vásquez also owned a cattle ranch on the lower San Pedro River.

Men congregate outside Leopold Ephraim's El Promontorio office in Nogales. The El Promontorio mine, at one time, employed 300 laborers. (Courtesy Rochlin Collection, Pimería Alta Historical Society.)

Ramón Vásquez, an early
Nogales businessman, owned
the Casa Colorado, or Red
House, as well as a cattle ranch.

He served as secretary and managing director of Compania Proveedora de Agua de Nogales S.A., an Arizona corporation that supplied Nogales, Sonora with water, and he served as president of Endowment Bank. In 1879, Vásquez married Carmen Soto, a descendant of a famous old Spanish family. Her grandfather had been commander-in-chief of the Tucson Presidio in the early days. The Vásquezes adopted two sons and one daughter.

Mark Lulley, born in Washington, D.C. on December 7, 1857, found prosperity in both mining and commercial ventures in Nogales. At age 18, he answered the siren call of Arizona emanating from tales of rich gold and silver strikes. He was soon joined by his brothers Moses and Louis. Lucky Lulley prospected in the Santa Rita Mountains where he discovered the Alto, the Warsaw, the Gold Tree, the Joplin, the Austerlitz, and the Wandering Jew. He also operated the Casino Bar, the Monte Carlo, and Lulley's Café and advertised gambling in his saloons as "all games on the square."

On a prospecting trip, he captured two bear cubs, intending to put them into the hands of an expert trainer who would teach them to dance. First, he included them in an elaborate wager on the outcome of the presidential election. Lulley, a member of the powerful New York Democratic organization, supported William Jennings Bryan in his 1901 campaign against William McKinley. Lulley promised that if Bryan won the election, he would ride from the capitol to the White House in a carriage pulled by a team of white horses. However, if Bryan lost, he would walk his bears from the capitol to the White House. McKinley won and Lulley traveled to Washington, D.C. to walk the inaugural parade along Pennsylvania

Avenue with his bears. McKinley honored Lulley at the White House and the bears were given to Washington Zoo.

Mark Lulley died in Arizona on October 12, 1916 of kidney failure. His remains were shipped by rail to Washington, D.C. where he was interred in the Washington Hebrew Congregation Cemetery at the request of his brother Moses. Little is known of Lulley's first wife. His second wife Manuela Lujan of Hermosillo was ostracized by her family for marrying a Jew. After Lulley's burial, she and her children returned to Tucson where she died in poverty in 1938.

Smuggling along the border generally involved opium, liquor, cattle, and Chinese, who were in great demand as railroad labor. The U.S. Customs Service began in 1880 with one man on horseback with headquarters at Nogales. Over the years, offices opened in Tucson, Phoenix, San Luis, Lukeville, Sasabe, Lochiel, Naco, and Douglas to collect duty on goods entering the United States and prevent contraband smuggling. Early collectors got $1,000 per year, and a mounted inspector received $3 per day with an additional dollar per day to feed his horse. When the railroad was completed, the Chinese opened restaurants, worked as gardeners, and operated laundries. Men who were out of work resented what they perceived as Chinese taking away their jobs. The U.S. Customs Department hired new agents designated specifically as Chinese Inspectors. One of the first Chinese Inspectors was also a member of the Arizona Rangers: Jeff Milton, age 26 and a good man with a gun, who patrolled the border from Douglas to Lukeville. The law had come to Nogales.

Mark Lulley, a miner and Nogales Jewish pioneer, captured two bears and walked in William McKinley's inaugural parade after betting on the outcome of the election. (Courtesy Abe Chanin.)

6. The Wedding of the Rails: 1881–1889

On October 25, 1882, the New Mexico & Arizona Railroad and the Sonora Railroad Ltd. met at the international border and life for Nogales changed. No longer would this be a community of rowdy saloons and border mercantiles. Now there would be sports, concerts, and church services. Doctors cared for patients and lawmen kept the peace. Teachers taught music along with reading, writing, and arithmetic. Merchants built new stores and carried a wider array of merchandise for both visitors and permanent residents. More people came and that meant more fires for the volunteer fire department.

William Raymond Morley had spent the previous June pushing Mexican rails from Guaymas ever closer and closer to Nogales. He had become discouraged with the lack of trained labor, the constant shortage of materials, and most of all the terrible heat of the Southwestern Desert. He wrote his wife Ada, "I want to see it out but will not spend another summer here." Morley, an engineer with the Santa Fe Railroad, surveyed the line from Guaymas, Sonora, through the Nogales Pass, and on to New Mexico. Santa Fe Railroad officials had successfully convinced Mexico's President Porfirio Díaz that this railroad line would help develop the west coast of Mexico as well as southern Arizona. Morley and his party traveled by wagon to Guaymas to construct the Sonora Railroad Ltd. line while other crews laid the rails from Benson, Arizona to connect with Sonora's northbound train.

Morley, orphaned at an early age, served in the 9th Iowa Volunteer Regiment as part of General William Tecumseh Sherman's army during the Civil War. During this period, he received training for building railroads. After his discharge, he entered Iowa State University and studied science and mathematics, but economic reasons intervened and he could not complete his degree. Morley became well known as a railroad engineer and, before long, the Atchison Topeka & Santa Fe Railroad (AT&SF) offered him a job. While the AT&SF built railroads in the West, Morley survived the railroad wars in Colorado and New Mexico. On July 4, 1879, he was named resident engineer in charge of all surveys west of the Rio Grande. While searching for a route from Mexico to Deming, New Mexico, he discovered

William Raymond Morley, here in 1881, engineered the early Nogales rail system. (Courtesy Pimería Alta Historical Society.)

a better one—a line directly north from Hermosillo, Sonora, to Nogales, Arizona, where the railroad could be served by a branch line from Benson, Arizona. Nogales showed its appreciation by naming its main street after Morley.

At a great celebration of the wedding of the rails on October 25, 1882, Nogales was arrayed with red, white, and blue bunting and flags. Ada McPherson Morley, who on that historic day wore a voluminous silk skirt and a bonnet decorated with flowers, was an accomplished pianist with all the fashionable graces of the time. She also served as president of the New Mexico Chapter of the Women's Christian Temperance Union and worked for women's suffrage.

The Benson locomotive was festooned from coalbin to smokestack with red, white, and blue bunting. Everywhere American flags whipped in the breeze. Then slowly with bells and whistles, the train came to a stop. Only inches from its cowcatcher waited the cowcatcher of the second train decorated with red, white, and green, the colors of Mexico. Morley, uncomfortable in a long frock coat and a silk stovepipe hat, listened while men made speeches in English and Spanish.

The crowd parted for a man who came forward with a rosewood box from which he removed a silver spike with inlaid gold plate, upon which was inscribed the date. Ada McPherson Morley, in the company of pioneers such as Jacob Isaacson and Leopold Ephraim, placed the spike in an already drilled hole and gave it a gentle tap, signifying that the last spike had been driven. Then the two cowcatchers ever so slowly moved forward and actually touched each other. A great shout of approval arose and a lady from Mexico cracked a bottle of champagne over the union.

After more speeches, it was on to dinner at Charles Sykes' grand hotel in Calabasas. Anticipating the coming of the railroad, Sykes built a two-story hotel on land, which was to be a vacation resort and a dude ranch. On the day of the wedding of the rails, 50 guests left Nogales by stagecoach and arrived for a five-course dinner. Sykes's hotel, described as one of the most exquisitely appointed in the West, operated for three years until Sykes turned it into his ranch headquarters and home. However, the land was part of an old land grant and Sykes fought a losing court battle to obtain clear title.

A few months after the wedding of the rails, Morley was chosen to locate a route for the Mexican Central Railroad and was named chief engineer. In January

Ada McPherson Morley held the honor of driving the last spike in the new railroad in 1882. (Courtesy Pimería Alta Historical Society.)

1883, while riding in a carriage, he remarked that a gun was placed in a dangerous position. The driver, in an effort to correct the situation, got tangled in the reins, setting off the gun and firing a bullet that pierced Morley's heart. He was dead at age 42.

Not long afterwards, the Southern Pacific negotiated with the Santa Fe regarding entry into California. The companies struck a deal wherein the Southern Pacific took over the rail line from Nogales to Guaymas and the Santa Fe took over the line from Needles to the new town of Barstow, California. For 16 years, the New Mexico & Arizona Railroad and the Sonora Railroad Ltd. from Guaymas, Sonora, Mexico, operated one passenger and one freight train each day going in both directions. One depot straddling the border served both railroads until 1898 when the U.S. Congress passed a law clearing a 60-foot strip along the border. After years of long-term leasing, the Southern Pacific purchased both the Mexican and the American lines. A new turntable, installed in 1907, serviced 20 locomotives during a 24-hour period. Switching cars in Nogales was a steam operation until 1950, although oil-burning locomotives had been in use since 1902. A 29-car icing platform was used to re-ice carloads of shrimp, melons, and

Charles P. Sykes threw a big party at his hotel in Calabasas to celebrate the wedding of the rails in 1882. After a long court battle, Sykes lost the land on which his hotel was built.

*The Hannah family
adorns a locomotive in
Nogales. In 1907, a new
turntable able to service
20 locomotives every
24 hours was installed.
(Courtesy Pimería Alta
Historical Society.)*

vegetables. In 1950, passenger service was discontinued. The federal government bought the Southern Pacific Station in 1963 and razed it to make room for the enlarged border crossing.

With the railroad came churches. The first minister to appear in Nogales was a Presbyterian, Reverend R.T. Liston, who came in response to a request by Congregationalists who were holding services in the public school in 1885. A year later, Reverend Liston broke ground for the Trinity Congregationalist Church. The Christian Endeavor Society of Boston had paid for their organ. A group of Methodists known as the Donnellyites, under Reverend John Donnelly, formed a commune at Sunnyside on the west side of the Huachucas. They made a fortune with the Copper Glance mine and it was without doubt the only Arizona mine where liquor and cussing were forbidden.

In 1887, Reverend Father Dolgt, the pastor at Tombstone, founded the Church of the Sacred Heart of Nogales. While Dolgt served Nogales as a missionary, he began erection of its first Roman Catholic church, a small adobe hall about 30 feet

63

by 22 feet, with two rooms that served as a residence for the visiting priest. After Dolgt, a series of priests served Nogales. Reverend Father Henry Granjon and Reverend Father Freri, who had come as French delegates of the Society of the Propagation of the Faith, served Mass from time to time. Both Fathers Delby and Gheldof maintained their official residences, but made extensive improvements in the Nogales church, paving the way for Reverend Father W. Meurer, who served as the first resident priest in Nogales from 1900 to 1905.

Sacred Heart grew under Father Louis Duval, who assumed charge of the church in 1905. The Right Reverend Monsignor Louis Duval, born in southern France on May 20, 1864, the son of Paul and Theresa Duval, studied at the Jesuit College at Avignon, France. In 1881, he began his preparation for the priesthood at St. Sulpice Seminary in Paris. Seven years later, in the diocese of Frejus, Duval was ordained to the priesthood and appointed to a professorship at St. Sulpice. In 1903, Bishop Henry Granjon, while on a visit to France, urged Duval to return to the United States with him and upon their arrival in Arizona, Duval was assigned to Prescott for one year. He returned to Tucson for five months before going to the church at Nogales. He served in Nogales until 1914 when he became a temporary rector of Tucson's St. Augustine's Cathedral, because Father John Timmerman could not leave Europe during World War I. In 1920, Duval returned to Nogales and, during the ensuing years, assisted the priests and people of Mexico whose churches were closed during Mexico's Revolution. Duval opened the first Nogales hospital under the direction of the Sisters of Mercy and, in 1910, he erected a new parochial school at Nogales.

John T. Brickwood, owner of the Exchange Saloon, built Brickwood Hotel in Nogales. Brickwood was born in Vandalia County, Illinois on October 19, 1849 and came west in 1867 and engaged in mining in Colorado. With $1,000 in his pocket, he moved to Prescott in 1868, where he went into a freighting business partnership for the United States Army at Fort Whipple. After a disagreement with his partner over a debt to a Mexican merchant in 1870, Brickwood sold out his interest in the business and moved to Tucson.

During a trip to Guaymas, Mexico, he paid the merchant $400 and cleared up the old debt. Brickwood became famous in northern Mexico when the merchant spread the story that he had paid a debt incurred by his partner. Brickwood became involved in several Mexican mining ventures and settled in Nogales. When Brickwood died in 1912, all the Nogales businesses, banks, and offices closed for half an hour.

Theodore Gebler, born in Berlin on July 1, 1831, received his education at a German military academy before learning the trade of tinsmith. At age 19, he came to the United States and worked as a tinsmith for about six years in New York. Here, in 1851, he married Louisa Waldman in New York and they had five children. The Geblers moved to San Francisco, where he owned a hardware store and served as a member of San Francisco's famous vigilante committee. In 1879, he took a pleasure trip to Arizona and made his permanent home in Nogales, where he operated a hardware store and served as a director of the First National

Bank. His wife and all five children preceded him in death and he died without heir in 1926. His will set aside funds for the construction of a building on Grand Avenue to care for the Nogales needy in perpetuity, a trust that still exists.

Manuel Escalada, born in northern Spain on April 11, 1867, emigrated to Brownsville, Texas at the age of 16, where he clerked in a mercantile. In 1892, he opened a Nogales dry goods store in partnership with his brother Leocadio. Escalada was active in the management of the business until his death and also served as a director of the Nogales Building and Loan Association. In September of 1899, he returned to Spain where he married Domitila Revuelta, and they became the parents of three sons, Jose, Luis, and Manuel. Escalada served as a member of the city council from 1918 to 1927. He was a director of the chamber of commerce from 1914 to 1927 and started the Nogales paving program. He contributed generously in time and money to Associated Charities, and when the news came of Manuel Escalada's death on June 6, 1927, it was said that he was everybody's friend. The Escalada and Gebler building still stands at 81–85 North Grand Avenue.

Theodore Gebler, an early Nogales businessman and philanthropist, learned the trade of tinsmith before moving to Nogales and serving as director of the First National Bank.

Ada EKey Jones arrived in Nogales in 1884 along with her parents, Mr. and Mrs. Robert EKey. Her father became the first Nogales superintendent of schools and an early Santa Cruz County recorder. Ada recalled that the family lived on a small ranch in a two-room house with a dirt floor, and that Nogales had two churches and a Wells Fargo office. Ada attended the Elm Street school in Nogales with her lifetime friends Katie Hill, Lula Reddock, Kittie Linder, Clara Holler, and Cordie and Julia Pearson. Lillie Chenoweth was the music teacher and Empara Mendez taught Spanish. Ada got her teaching certificate and taught school with a few books, slates, chalk, and a blackboard in a building that the Congregationalists used as a church. Ada said they precipitated a "church organ fuss" when the congregation insisted on taking its organ to its new quarters. The public school trustees took a notion to enforce the school truancy law and compel all Mexican children to attend school. Ada recalled that they were holding school everywhere—in the rear of the El Paso Store, in the theater building, and in Marsh's Hall.

One of Ada's Mexican students was Abelardo Rodríguez, who served as Mexico's president from 1932 to 1934. Before becoming president, Rodríguez had been a professional baseball player, and through farming and gambling operations in Baja California he became one of the 12 richest men in Mexico. Whether he was a good student is debatable because his countrymen said he spoke English poorly and Spanish even worse.

Ada EKey, an early Nogales schoolteacher, remembers holding school in church buildings, theaters, and the back of the El Paso Store. (Courtesy Pimería Alta Historical Society.)

In 1896, the Nogales Young Ladies' Mandolin Club posed for this picture. Other extracurricular activities included a Dramatic Club and an Athletic Club. (Courtesy Pimería Alta Historical Society.)

By 1897, there were 36 public schools and 42 teachers in the greater Nogales area. The Lochiel school, in use until 1973, has been kept intact as a testament to history. Washington Camp had telephone, no electricity, and no plumbing as late as the 1920s. Its children brought their lunches in lard pails or in square Prince Albert cans. At one school, the teacher's chair had no bottom, but was padded with a subscription to the *New York Times*.

Ada EKey Jones recalled that the young women of the town formed a Dramatic Club and presented the play *Ten Nights in a Bar*. The proceeds were used to buy trees for the park. The young men formed an Athletic Club that gave informal dances every two weeks in the rear of the International Drug Store, which was just large enough for three sets of quadrille. The young women also formed a mandolin club.

In 1895, Nogales held a three-day Mardi Gras, which was promoted by the Athletic Club. The closing event featured a parade staged on flat cars, with each car representing a distinct period of time. The cars were drawn from the Nogales roundhouse across the line to a grand ball in the Mexican Customs House where the large freight room had been cleaned and decorated. A fine Mexican band provided the music and the young men broke cascarones, eggs full of scented

Emitia Gotsis was crowned queen of this early Nogales Mardi Gras celebration. Accompanying her are Elsa Oseta and Carlota Oseta. (Courtesy Pimería Alta Historical Society.)

confetti, over the girls' heads and by the next morning, the confetti was an inch deep.

Nogales, Arizona faced a problem when it ordained a dog tax. Serious trouble was anticipated as the Mexicans were very partial to their dogs because it was not fair to expect the dogs to observe the niceties of international treaties by not traipsing across the border where American officials might pick them up. Everyone sighed with relief when Nogales, Sonora passed a similar ordinance and requested that their dog tags be inspected on the United States side of the border, and the two cities agreed that dog tags should be mutually respected, regardless of nationality. Once again, an international incident was averted.

Newspapers are the memory of a town because they chronicle the lives of its citizens. Fortunately, Nogales had several early newspapers that also espoused the political views of their publishers. John G. Ginn established the weekly *Frontier* in 1855. A year later, Judge M.B. Crawford published the *Frontier* and, in 1887, his wife was listed as the "editress." In 1888, George C. Peck of the *Tombstone Epitaph* purchased the Nogales *Frontier*. In 1886, *El Monitor Fronterizo* was published both in English and Spanish and lasted seven years. Allen T. Bird, veteran of the Civil War, miner, and journalist, moved *The Oasis* from Benson to Nogales in 1894. He wrote that the front door of his new premises faced the Territory of Arizona while the back gate was in the state of Sonora. Thus, in case any libelous or slanderous material appeared in the paper, it could be ignored by claiming residence in the most convenient country.

Bird was born in Madison, Wisconsin, April 13, 1849, to Elizabeth and Rhenodyne A. Tracy, natives of New York and pioneer Wisconsin families. His grandfather H.H. Bird, a contractor and builder, secured the contract to erect the state capitol building when Wisconsin separated from Iowa. From his father he learned the printer's trade. At age 15, Bird enlisted in the 141st Infantry Regiment to fight in the Civil War. He was mustered out at the end of the war with a good military record and resumed his interrupted education. In Omaha, Nebraska, he worked as a printer on the *Omaha Republican*. Tiring of the newspaper business, Bird went to work for the railroad. He became a ticket agent for the Union Pacific at Cheyenne, Wyoming after working as a brakeman, baggageman, and conductor. In 1880, he began a career as a miner in California, Arizona, and Mexico City. He rode the Canadian border for more than 20,000 miles on horseback in pursuit of mining interests. With the love of writing never far from his heart, Bird wrote and published the *Land of Nayarit*, under the auspices of the Arizona and Sonora Chambers of Commerce.

Before moving to Nogales in 1884, Bird published the *San Bernardino Daily Index*. In his newspaper columns and speeches, he advocated women's suffrage for Arizona and his wife Calla Nabb served on a committee for women's votes.

Allen T. Bird was an early Nogales newspaperman and accomplished writer. Bird was also a veteran of the Civil War and a former railroad employee.

In 1895, he received a commission in Company G of the First Regiment Infantry of the National Guard of Arizona to serve as Arizona Governor Myron H. McCord's aide-de-camp with the rank of lieutenant colonel. After he completed this assignment, Bird went on to work for seven years as clerk of the Santa Cruz County District Court. He also served as United States Commissioner at Nogales and as director of the Nogales Chamber of Commerce. When transcontinental tariffs were formed, the New York commission relegated Nogales to the position of an intermediate point to a branch line point, which added 49¢ per hundred weight on all eastern freight entering Nogales. The chamber of commerce sent a committee, with Bird as chairman, to San Francisco to persuade the railroad to file a supplementary schedule that restored Nogales to its former place in the transcontinental system, saving the Nogales merchants about $50,000 annually.

James J. Chatham, born in Terre Haute, Indiana on October 21, 1848, moved with his family to Illinois, where he attended public schools. At age 20, he worked as a Kansas farmer while learning the printer's trade. He was city constable at Olathe, Kansas before moving to Kansas City, where he was a telegraph editor for the *Kansas City Times*. In May 1863, Chatham established the Kansas *Coffeville Courier* and, in 1877, he sold the paper and accepted the position of sergeant at arms for the Kansas House of Representatives. In Joplin, Missouri, Chatham became associated with the Joplin Press and published with the *Daily Republican*. A year later, he went to Cherryvale, Kansas, to run the *Globe* until February 12, 1882, when he moved to Arizona to work for the *Tucson Citizen* for three years. He edited the Tombstone *Epitaph* before moving to Nogales to publish the *Daily Reserve*. In

Friends and family from both sides of the border celebrated Mardi Gras at this Nogales Sonora Custom House.

Cordie Pearson and Lillie Chatham were just two of the young ladies in Nogales society. (Courtesy Pimería Alta Historical Society.)

1888, he founded the Nogales *Sunday Herald*. Chatham won election to the 15th Arizona legislature on the Republican ticket while serving as Nogales postmaster and school trustee. After 1908, he was elected justice of the peace and coroner. In 1891, Chatham married Lillian Chenoweth and they had five children.

With the influx of people, Nogales had to form a volunteer fire department. In 1895, Leander W. Mix of the Independent Hose Company in Nogales authorized the purchase of a hand-drawn, hand-operated hook-and-ladder cart, and a hose cart and pumper affectionately known as "Able and Willing," which is now on display at the Pimería Alta Historical Society. The pumper, which was retired in 1917, functioned by drawing water from Nogales's cisterns and wells, and spraying it under pressure with several firemen grasping a rail on each side. Any fireman whose dues were unpaid was not allowed to operate the hose. When Nogales built a new firehouse with a tower for a bell to alert the firemen, the city got rid of its earlier alarm system of firing shots into the air to warn of a fire.

In 1910, Bracey Curtis, president of the National Bank, became the Nogales fire chief and oversaw the construction of a combined town hall and fire station, and its dedication on February 15, 1915. This building is now the home of the Pimería Alta Historical Society. Two years later, the fire department acquired its first motorized piece of equipment, an American La France hose-and-ladder

Leander W. Mix of the Independent Hose Company was Nogales's first fire chief. Mix authorized the purchase of "Able and Willing," a hose cart and pumper.

truck. Nogales, Arizona and Nogales, Sonora entered into a mutual agreement to help each other in case of fire. Today, Arizona equipment no longer crosses the international line, but it still attaches a hose to a water line to increase the pressure. In 1920, Nogales established a Public Safety Department with three paid firemen, Alfred Camerlin, William Lowe, and John Bachelier. This department existed until 1977 when the police and fire departments were separated in a city referendum. In 1921, an alarm was installed on the firehouse roof and the nighttime fireman slept in a new loft. In case of fire, he was charged with answering the telephone, sounding the alarm, and driving the fire engine to the fire. Later, a siren was installed and in recent years this has been replaced by a radio communications system.

As the town grew, so did its medical community. Dr. William F. Chenoweth began his surgery practice in 1889. Born in Ross County, Ohio, on September 15, 1865 to Dr. A.L. and Emma Kelley Chenoweth, he studied medicine at the University of Cincinnati and received his doctorate in medicine in 1888. He practiced in Cincinnati for one year before coming to Nogales. Chenoweth also served as the superintendent of health for Santa Cruz County and as a surgeon for the Southern Pacific Railroad.

Bracey Curtis, Nogales fireman and businessman, became fire chief in 1910 and was responsible for the construction of a combined town hall and fire station.

Dr. Adolphus H. Noon, physician, mine developer, and politician, was born in London in 1838. At age 15, he enlisted in the British military and traveled to South Africa to study medicine under Dr. John Eglinton, an East Indian surgeon. Noon married Emma Slaughter, a native of England. In 1865, Adolphus and his wife emigrated to America where he headed for Nebraska because the railroad workers needed a doctor. He then moved to San Francisco where he attended the College of Physicians and Surgeons. Here Captain John J. Noon, no relation, told Adolphus of the wonderful climate in the border country of the Arizona Territory. The family moved to Nogales. Besides his medical talents, Noon developed the Oro Blanco gold district. He served on the first Santa Cruz County board of supervisors, was clerk of the district court, and was elected the first representative to the territorial legislature on the Democratic ticket. From 1910 to 1911, Noon served as mayor of Nogales. The Noon family has educated five generations at the University of Arizona in fields of medicine, law, engineering, agriculture, and music. These were just a few of the hardy pioneers who sowed the seeds of civilization on a harsh frontier.

7. Federal Land Grant Problems: 1890s

The railroad brought more permanent settlers who required a larger variety of businesses and social services. However, in 1893, Congress demonetized silver and the mines closed when the prices dropped. Fortunately, Nogales prospectors still found gold on both sides of the border. That same year, the Pima County Board of Supervisors signed incorporation papers for Nogales on July 21. Still, Nogalians were not satisfied because most of them had not been able to attend the session because of flooding in the Santa Cruz Valley. The sympathetic supervisors repeated the hearing on July 22. The First Nogales town council included Theodore Gebler, James B. Mix, Anton Proto, George B. Marsh, and Edward B. Hogan. The council elected Mix as mayor. Nogales borrowed $2,000 from Gebler for operating expenses and bought an official seal.

Law enforcement still depended on citizens taking matters into their own hands. Frank King arrived to edit the *Border Vidette,* and he and Allen Bird from the *Oasis* kept up a lively repartee of divergent opinions in their editorials. By accident, King stumbled into a bank robbery in 1894, when members of the notorious Black Jack gang burst into the International Bank where the clerk was counting out money. When the outlaws heard the door open, they grabbed $30,000, but in their efforts to flee, they tripped over each other and dropped the money. In the meantime, King exchanged shots with the outlaws who were waiting outside. The clumsy robbers rode hard out of town firing at anything in their line of sight. The bank clerk grabbed a gun, shot a hole in the ceiling, and killed a horse hitched to a woodcutter's wagon. King tried to jump on a nearby buggy horse, but it threw him off. He took a horse from a passing cowboy, who thought he was a robber and he caught up with the gang in a canyon. But seeing that he was dangerously out-gunned, he returned to Nogales. The gang made their getaway, but the bank recovered its money.

Culture came to Nogales with the Nogales Opera House and concerts and productions by the Dramatic Association. Young ladies loved invitations to the monthly socials sponsored by the Young Men's Athletic Association. James Mix ordered a music box from New York and provided the music.

Santa Cruz County's second incorporated town, Patagonia, was founded in 1896 by rancher Rollin R. Richardson, who persuaded the railroad that an ore-loading dock and stockyards would be more convenient for shippers at present-day Patagonia than at the Crittenden station. Grumbling residents moved their homes board by board and their personal belongings more than 2 miles to the present-day site. When Richardson proposed to call the new town Rollin, the townsfolk rebelled and called it Patagonia.

Frank Duffy, one of the leading Arizona attorneys, arrived in Nogales in 1893 to accept a clerkship with the U.S. Customs Service. During his spare time, he read law to pass the bar. His career included service as county assessor, district attorney, Nogales city attorney and member of the city council. In 1911, he was elected to the bench of the superior court.

Nogales faced a serious problem of land ownership during this period. Little did they realize that their fate would be determined by a slave child born on

William "Black Jack" Christian led a gang of outlaws into Nogales to rob a bank, only to panic and drop the $30,000. (Courtesy Arizona Historical Society.)

March 21, 1856. On that pleasant spring day in Thomasville, Georgia, only a slight air of tension permeated the Reverend Reuben Luckey's humble slave quarters. The birth of a black slave baby was no particular cause for concern other than as a piece of property. While the women went about their work, they comforted Isabella Buckhalter, whose time had arrived. It was her first child, and her husband Festus Flipper Sr. had gone to Virginia with his owner Ephraim G. Ponder. The baby, Henry Ossian Flipper, would become West Point's first African-American graduate and his career would have a profound effect on Nogales in the Arizona Territory.

In Nogales, Flipper forged his career as an engineer, Spanish translator, Justice Department special agent, inventor, author, historian, and newspaper editor. While serving as special agent to the Court of Private Land Claims, he saved thousands of acres of Arizona land from falling into the hands of unscrupulous speculators. Flipper arrived in Nogales in October 1885 and was listed in the newspaper as among the distinguished arrivals. He had been court-martialed and dismissed from the military after funds in his possession were missing. Two years later, he purchased a town lot for $28 in Mexican money. In 1889, Flipper purchased a second piece of Nogales property for $25 in Mexican money on what is now Nelson Avenue. He wrote Festus that people in Nogales were not so prejudiced and mean as they were in the south. He formed close friendships

The appearance of the international border at Nogales changed in 1897 after Congress declared a 60-foot strip to be free of all businesses. Now it was only operable as a public highway. (Courtesy Pimería Alta Historical Society.)

with men such as Jesse Grant, a son of President Ulysses Grant, whose home still stands on Crawford Street, and James J. Chatham, newspaper publisher and Nogales postmaster, and George Christ.

The townsfolk of Nogales held no legal title to their homes, and their lands were claimed by the Camou and Elías families, along with several litigants who had purchased quit-claims from the Camou-Elías interests. After the surrender of Geronimo, economic activity increased in southern Arizona. New mining claims were filed. Ranchers grazed their cattle on lands granted to them by the Spanish and Mexican governments prior to the Gadsden Purchase.

When the U.S. government accepted the Gadsden Purchase treaty, it agreed to recognize the legality of land grants that had been acquired during the periods when this region was either a part of New Spain or Mexico, provided certain conditions were met. Grants had to have been located and duly recorded in the archives of Mexico, and had to be marked with proper monuments of mortar and stone. Land reverted to public domain if the property was abandoned for more than three years. An exception was made if it could be proved that the land was deserted because of Native American depredations. Documents used to determine the validity of the titles in Mexico were bound in two volumes known as the *Toma de Razón,* or the "accounts of the people of reason."

In 1891, Congress created a special Court of Private Land Claims with sessions to be held in Denver and Santa Fe to determine the validity of claims in New Mexico and Arizona. A year later, a separate district was established in Tucson to hear the Arizona claims. President Benjamin Harrison appointed five judges. Other court officials included U.S. Prosecutor Matthew Reynolds, U.S. Attorney James H. Reeder, U.S. Attorney General Richard Olney, Clerk Ireneo Chaves, Deputy Clerk R.L. Long, and U.S. Marshal E.L. Hall. Will Tipton and Henry Flipper served as special agents.

Long tedious searching and translation of documents located in Hermosillo and Mexico City depositories complicated the adjudication of land grant validity. Measurements such as *sitios, cabellarias,* and *varas* had to be interpreted in English units. Flipper was complimented by judges and government officials, not only for his translation of text, but also for incorporating the subtle nuances of the Spanish language.

Procedures for conveying grants were the same under Spanish and Mexican rule. The *matriz,* or original document, was filed in the appropriate government repository. The most common document accepted by the court as evidence of a land grant was the *expediente,* or second original. This paper had to be in the possession of the claimant. A *testimonio,* or second copy, was allowed if it could be authenticated.

While the Los Nogales de Elías grant was argued in court, Nogales Mayor W.F. Overton held the town folk titles in trust until the ownership question could be resolved. This grant, if it had been allowed, would have given the claimants the entire town of Nogales. Nogales residents hired Flipper to search their land records and he determined that by taking the well-defined monuments at the

Part of the Elías family involved in the Nogales land grant suit is shown here. (Courtesy Arizona Historical Society.)

south end of the alleged grant and making a survey in accordance with grant terms, the claim not only failed to take in the town of Nogales, but missed the international border by approximately 1 mile. Armed with this information, Nogales residents prosecuted the Camou-Elías claim in the Court of Private Land Claims in Tucson on August 15, 1892.

The populace of Nogales expressed complete confidence in Flipper's ability through their newspapers, and they were delighted with his appointment as special agent to the Court of Private Land Claims. The Nogales *Oasis* reported:

> Lieut. H.O. Flipper has been appointed by the government as its agent
> to take testimony for it in the land grant cases. Being a thorough Spanish
> scholar and knowing the Spanish laws by intent as well as text he will be
> invaluable to all concerned.

Flipper's duties included translating Spanish documents as well as Spanish and Mexican laws dating from the sixteenth century, and conducting new surveys under the mandates of those documents. During his years of surveying in Mexico, he determined which lands were under private title and which were in public domain by examining thousands of grants in Chihuahua and Sonora. Through personal acquaintance with Mexican officials, he had ready access to government documents.

Flipper was paid $10 a day plus expenses. However, from November to April 1893, he received no compensation when Washington bureaucrats turned down his claims because in their opinion, $10 a day was exorbitant. When his claim for working on Sunday bounced, Matt Reynolds defended Flipper's necessity for working on the Sabbath because the materials had to be ready for a court date. When a Chinese man signed his meal receipts and no one in Washington could read it, Flipper's voucher bounced even though the hotel owner countersigned it.

Attorney General Richard Olney asked Reynolds if someone other than Flipper could be hired to perform these services, presumably because of his color and military record. Reynolds staunchly defended his choice and Olney relented, but urged Reynolds to keep Flipper's expenses to a minimum. While most Nogalians supported Flipper, those who were suing for land grants had every reason to want him fired. From time to time, Flipper served as deputy postmaster when Postmaster James.J. Chatham went out of town. When postal funds turned up missing, the land grant claimants saw their opportunity to get rid of both Chatham and Flipper. They brought Flipper's court-martial to the attention of the governor of Arizona, and accused him of complicity with Chatham in the missing postal funds.

The land grant trial continued and attorney Rochester Ford produced a document purported to be a copy of the grant record from the *Toma de Razón* for the Elías interests. Flipper served as the only government witness. When U.S. Attorney Parker offered Flipper's resurvey of the lands in question, Ford objected on the basis that it was irrelevant, incompetent, and of an entirely different ranch. Flipper had indeed resurveyed the Elías ranch in Sonora because their Arizona claim was derived from the northern points of this ranch. When Reynolds asked Flipper if he had recomputed the land area based on his new survey, Ford shouted "irrelevant, immaterial and incompetent." Flipper continued to testify that all of the original grant was located in Mexico. He proceeded in a composed manner, even though his answers were interrupted by Ford's shouts of "objection!" Finally, the judges silenced Ford, who announced that for the record he objected to all of Flipper's testimony. Flipper confirmed that he had made all the measurements and calculations himself and the most dramatic moment came when he described an alleged north monument, which would determine whether the grant spilled over the border and beyond the townsite of Nogales:

> Well I don't think it is a monument at all: I don't think it ever was. It looks more like an ant-hill. About twenty steps from it in a northeast direction is another exactly like it . . . They are recent monuments beyond any question . . . I never saw any monuments like that anywhere in Mexico.

For all his protests, Ford asked Flipper very few questions on cross-examination. The tedium of the closing speeches alone would have been enough to cause any tribunal to make a quick ruling. Ford presented the defendants' cases by speaking all of Tuesday afternoon and part of Wednesday morning. George Hill Howard followed and spoke till noon. Selim Franklin followed and spoke four hours until court took a merciful adjournment. He resumed his speech the next morning and spoke for another hour.

Prosecutor Reynolds claimed that the alleged transcript on which defendants based their claim only professed to be a copy of an original private paper in the possession of José Elías and was "fraudulent, null and void." The judges took 30 minutes to rule that the entire grant lies south of the border. From the Nogalians' point of view, arguments for the defendants were weak, while those of the government were brilliant and to the point.

On December 24, 1893, Flipper sent the *Nogales Herald* a telegram from Tucson stating, "The court decides in our favor." The town went wild with joy. In spite of drizzling rain, the band came out and residents set off firecrackers. It was the best Christmas present for Nogales and the revelry carried on until Friday morning.

The Nogales *Oasis* proclaimed "Long Live Flipper!" and "Here is how it was done!" The *Oasis* reported that even though Judge Stone had his nose smashed in the Lordsburg train wreck, his head was all right. Now the residents could

Henry Ossian Flipper was the first African-American graduate of the United States Military Academy at West Point. (Courtesy United States Military Academy at West Point.)

acquire perfect titles to their homes and businesses. On Friday evening, all Nogales businesses closed at 6 p.m., when the citizens turned out to welcome the stagecoach that carried Flipper, Louis Proto, and other members of the Protective Association Committee. The streets were crowded and everyone had their electric light bulbs turned on. In the Montezuma Hotel, preparations were underway for a celebratory banquet.

At 8:30 that evening, 20 gentlemen filed into the brilliantly arranged dining room and sat down to the finest supper that was ever gotten up in Nogales. Claret and black coffee were the only beverages served, but they sufficed for the purpose of drinking to the health of all those who aided in winning the glorious victory for the people. For Flipper, the celebration was marred by racism. One doctor declared he would not eat at the same table with a "Negro." Later, when the same doctor was running for the position of a school trustee, Flipper worked for the other candidate, who "beat this Negro-hating doctor by a good majority."

Flipper furnished the laws and information that knocked out the land grants in Arizona. But no sooner was the celebration over than he was removed from his position as special agent and accused of complicity in the disappearance of postal funds. Except for the land grant claimants, everyone in Nogales believed that Flipper and Postmaster J.J. Chatham were innocent of the defalcation of postal funds. The Tombstone *Epitaph* wrote that the charge against Flipper was because "he is a colored man." However, the opinion in Nogales was that he was "too well posted" to suit the land grant claimants.

Land grant claimants attempted to discredit Flipper by accusing him of collusion in the embezzlement. Petitions, signed by businesses and individuals, assailed the Justice Department in an effort to have Flipper reinstated. What emerged was an obvious conspiracy involving U.S. Marshal William K. Meade, Acting Arizona Governor Charles M. Bruce, and Louis Strother, who had replaced Flipper as quartermaster at Fort Davis, along with the various land claimants. In a letter to Bruce, Strother said that Flipper's court-martial panel believed him to be guilty of embezzlement, but showed sympathy by finding him guilty of only one charge. The governor turned this letter over to Marshal Meade:

> As the interest of both the settlers and land claimants are very large it would be very questionable, it seems to me to leave them in the hands of a man of bad character, whose past record is such as to destroy all respect that should be entertained for an official holding such a responsible position; and whose standing in Arizona at the present continues to be a very disreputable one.

Meade turned the letters from Bruce and Strother over to Attorney General Richard Olney who insisted that Flipper be removed as special agent until the case was cleared up. Reynolds was determined that the land claimants not be allowed to dictate to the government who should collect its evidence. It had come to his attention that Colin Cameron had attempted to corrupt Flipper.

Cameron, a rancher who claimed the San Rafael de la Zanja grant, stood accused of fraudulently acquiring his land and had every reason to resent Flipper. Flipper stated that Cameron's title was a forgery, and that if anyone had claim to this land it would be the residents of the town of Santa Cruz. A letter from Judge William H. Barnes saved Flipper's job and accused Marshal Meade of slander. In Barnes's opinion, the only reason the marshal maintained his position was because he hired a bookkeeper who kept him honest. Otherwise, he was an ignorant, egotistic, and malicious man who was *persona non grata* in the Democratic party. He wrote:

> Meade has been for years a willing instrument to do anything the Land Grabbers want. Is a tool of the conspirators. On yesterday before the decision of the court was announced, he was very confident that the Government would be defeated and he joined with Colin Cameron to bet a bottle of wine that the grant claimants would win the case.

Chatham's case was ignored by the Grand Jury and Flipper was reinstated. The Nogales de Elías claimants took their case all the way to the U.S. Supreme Court. On April 9, 1898, Flipper boarded the train for Washington, D.C. to defend his work on the Los Nogales de Elías claim before the U.S. Supreme Court. The Nogales *Oasis* was upset when Santiago Ainsa, attorney for the land grant claimants, had the "gall" to assail Flipper's credibility. They were happy to report that the reply to this assault by Matt Reynolds was a "eulogy of Mr. Flipper's worth and character of which the many friends of the gentleman are very proud." The U.S. Supreme Court rendered a favorable ruling on the Nogales de Elías claim to the people of Nogales. U.S. Attorney Richard Olney, commenting on Flipper, said the following:

> My investigation as to Mr. Flipper, and my subsequent observations of him, as well as my associations with the people of Arizona, justify me in stating that no successful attack can be made on his honesty, his integrity, and his reliability and this is borne out by the general respect and esteem accorded him in the community where he lives and where these land grants are situated.

Flipper continued his work on southern Arizona land grants with the support of the people. His next project was the San Rafael de Valle land grant, a small claim that caused big trouble in Santa Cruz County. This four-sitio grant, in the lovely San Pedro Valley, was acquired by Rafael Elías in 1827 for $240. Apache depredations forced Elías to leave, but when he died, his widow Guadalupe and their three sons José Juan, Manuel, and José María were in possession of the land. In 1862, the family took out a $12,000 mortgage, financed by the Camou brothers, Joseph Pierre and Pascual of Hermosillo, Sonora, on a portion of their land. The Camou's attorney William Herring sued for foreclosure on the land. He took the

Henry Ossian Flipper, here at age 44 in Nogales, became embroiled in the Los Nogales de Elías land claim. (Courtesy Arizona Historical Society.)

land grant case to the Supreme Court where Flipper was once again required to testify for the government. Herring never disputed Flipper's translations or his statements as to the conditions of the grant. Instead, he attempted to discredit Flipper's testimony by making him guess the distances from one point to another. The *Arizona Enterprise,* furious at Herring for belittling Flipper, reported that Herring's mind evidently was not as big as himself, because its true size and capacity appeared when he indulged in a "disgusting harangue of vituperation against a competent officer."

Herring told what he considered a witty story of an ass, which the newspaper said would have been better received in a Bowery dive. The story would have met a less disgusting reception if Herring had stated that he himself figured as the ass in that story. According to the *Enterprise*, the knowledge displayed in the conduct of this case by the "eminent counsel (Herring) would indicate that he is still the ass." The Court of Private Land Claims rejected this claim on the basis that an edict with dictator Santa Anna was illegal and subject to review by the central government in Mexico and the United States. The U.S. Supreme Court ruled that a temporary dictator did not nullify the grant.

The Justice Department asked Flipper to examine the Santo Ignacio de Babocomari grant translation, and he said "that it was as poor a translation as he ever saw." However, the defense attorneys fought Flipper bitterly, charging that he had worked for the Mexican government while he was in Sonora. Flipper strongly denied the accusation:

> for which I had received $1500, that I then returned to Nogales, got drunk and remained drunk until all the money was gone. These charges were investigated, but every man, woman and child in Nogales knew I never drank liquor and proved the charges false in every particular.

Flipper's marriage contract in 1891 with Luisa Montoya is one of the more unusual documents in Arizona history. However, he never mentioned her in any of his writings. Until 1959, Arizona miscegenation laws prohibited persons of different races from marrying. Any person solemnizing a racially mixed marriage was meted the same punishment as the persons getting married. The marriage contract, signed by Flipper and Luisa Montoya and witnessed by George Christ and Henry M. Stanley, prominent citizens from Nogales, reads in part:

Luisa Montoya from Nogales entered into a marriage contract with Henry O. Flipper even though racially mixed marriages were prohibited. (Courtesy Arizona Historical Society.)

> That the full name of said part of the first part is Henry Ossian Flipper . . .
> That the full name of said second party is Louisa [*sic*] Montoya . . . That
> first and second parties do hereby jointly make this their declaration
> of marriage . . . That said parties do hereby agree to take each other as
> husband and wife and to live together as such from the date hereof . . .
> That their marriage has not been solemnized, but this declaration of
> marriage is made in lieu of such Solemnization. Witness our hands and
> seals this 10th day of September 1891.

Flipper's "marriage" evidently did not last long because, less than a year later, he wrote his brother Festus that he was still a bachelor, "and I have never seen any other woman out this way, colored, white or Mexican, that I would give a fin for as a wife. All the nice girls are back east where you are." In the same letter, he described the hard times in Nogales. Everywhere tramps begged for something to eat or some work. He blamed the Democrats for the demonetization of silver and the hard times, and described himself as a Republican "first, last, and all the time." By now, Flipper had put on a little weight and wore glasses.

Flipper by his own admission helped fix a Nogales election, but this was a common Arizona sport at the time. D. Altschul, chairman of the local Republican committee, was running for delegate to the Constitutional Convention. While calling for an election of delegates, Altschul had the ballots printed with his name at the top. On election day Flipper, Jesse Grant, and James J. Chatham, plotted to defeat Altschul just for the fun of it. First, they decided to print up their own ballots, but then Flipper came up with a superior strategy. He and Grant set out in opposite directions to collect Altschul's ballots. The first man Flipper met was Altschul, who gave him a "big bunch" of ballots. Back in the office, they scratched out Altschul's name and wrote in Chatham's. The upshot was that Chatham won, and Altschul was so humiliated that he sold his Nogales property and went to South America to raise sugar.

While Chatham served his term as a delegate to the Constitutional Convention, he appointed Flipper as editor of the *Nogales Sunday Herald*. Thus, Flipper became the first black editor of a white newspaper and had a lot of fun doing it. In December of 1895, Flipper surveyed the lines of the corporation limits of Nogales. He discovered that the line ran right through the homes of many residents, including that of Mayor Fred Herrera. The Nogales city council paid Flipper $20 in gold for this town survey. Flipper spent much of 1896 surveying routes for roads in Mexico. That same year, he received notice in January of his appointment as Deputy U.S. Mineral Surveyor. He took out an advertisement in the *Nogales Oasis*:

> Henry O. Flipper—U.S. Deputy Mineral Surveyor. Mine and Land
> Surveys in United States or Mexico. Thorough acquaintance with
> Mexican and Land and Mining Laws. Translations in English and
> Spanish. Notary Public.

This Nogales political rally featured a hot air balloon. (Courtesy Pimería Alta Historical Society.)

The *Oasis* assured its readers that the requirement to post a bond of $20,000 was "simply to guarantee that he will not survey your ore body over into the adjoining claim owned by someone else."

On a trip to Tucson, Flipper ran into a former West Point classmate, Robert D. Read, who was now a captain in command of the 10th cavalry. When Flipper sat down to dinner at the San Xavier Hotel, Read promptly got up and left without eating. During this period, Flipper received a patent for an improved tent made from one piece of material that could be "expeditiously and conveniently erected." It was designed to be carried by two men, but provided shelter for four.

Although Nogales adored Flipper, this did not deter him from reprimanding the *Oasis* newspaper if he thought it necessary. Flipper called attention to an error in the paper regarding mineral rights on land grants. The Court of Private Land Claims specifically exempted from confirmation any claim to minerals on private land claims, except where such minerals were provided for in the grant itself by Spain or Mexico. Flipper suggested that the editor read the act of March 3, 1891, and warned that grant claimants were fighting for "outer boundaries" in order to control water and crush out small holders.

When his work was complete with the Court of Private Land Claims in 1901, Flipper received a telegram from the Balvanera Mining Company in Ocampo, Chihuahua asking him for a meeting in El Paso. The president of the company, William McAdoo, offered Flipper the position of resident engineer. When the Mexican Revolution wreaked havoc along the border, once again Flipper's work situation became unstable.

In the 1880s, another important government office appeared in Nogales, that of the United States Customs Service. By law, all importers had to report their imports at the custom house at Nogales, Arizona's port of entry and the headquarters for the Arizona district. That is not to say all items enter the United States legally. George Christ, who served as the first collector of customs, received $2,000 per year. A deputy collector received $1,000 per year and a mounted inspector of the Customs Patrol received $3 per day plus $1 per day for horse feed. One early collector took a shipment of gold and fled to Mexico, never to be heard from again. In addition to collecting customs duties, the Customs Service is charged with the prevention of smuggling. Today, it is drugs, but in the 1880s, Chinese were smuggled into the United States as railroad laborers. Nogales also received a telephone franchise during this era, but when the town clerk received the first outrageously expensive bill of $3, the telephone was promptly removed. In 1962, Nogales installed special equipment so it could dial direct to Nogales, Sonora, a service unique in the United States.

George Christ, a friend of Henry Ossian Flipper, became Nogales's first collector of customs. (Courtesy Pimería Alta Historical Society.)

8. Creation of Santa Cruz County: 1899

As Nogales turned the last century, it saw progress and problems. The depression of 1893 shut off eastern investments, the silver devaluation closed down many mines, and an extended drought forced ranchers to sell their cattle at a loss or watch them die. Gold and copper continued to play an important part in Nogales's economy and boom towns sprung up over night. In 1873, while working as a rancher in the San Pedro valley, Indian Agent Thomas Jeffords asked Davis Tecumseh Harshaw to take his stock off the Chiricahua Apache lands. When Harshaw moved them to Durasno near Nogales, he located a couple of small mine sites in a place he called Harshaw. By 1880, the Hermosa Mining Company erected a 20-stamp mill at his mines and, for two years, Harshaw prospered. The town boasted a population of 2,000, a variety of stores, lodging houses, numerous saloons, hotels, and a newspaper, the *Arizona Bullion*. However, in 1882, damaging storms and a fire forced the closing of the mine. In 1887, Harshaw was reborn on a much smaller scale. Approximately 100 residents lived there and limited mining continued until 1909, when Harshaw once again became a ghost town. A second rebirth, brought about by mining in the area by ASARCO, lasted from 1937 to 1956.

Duquesne and Washington Camp have always been geographically and industrially tied closely together. Washington Camp was first settled in the 1870s and, 20 years later, the Duquesne Mining and Reduction Company of Pittsburgh purchased the property. The company established its headquarters at Duquesne and built a reduction plant in Washington Camp. Thomas Shane and N.H. Capen founded the Bonanza Mine in the 1880s and sold their claim to a Mr. Hensley in 1889, who in turn sold it to the Duquesne Company the same year. For a few years, the towns of Duquesne and Washington Camp were headquarters for more than 80 mining claims covering 1,600 acres. Both towns prospered and reached their peak populations of around 1,000 by 1900. Today, a few people still live in the area and those who enjoy ghost towns will find several old buildings, including the ruins of a school and a boarding house.

In 1873, the *Tucson Citizen* reported that mining activity had taken place so early near Oro Blanco that some huge oak trees had grown up on the scene of obvious mining activity. When gold mining resumed, the mine lay so close to the international boundary that the property had to be resurveyed to prove that it lay within the border of the United States. Early mining towns had their fair share of crime and taxed the resources of lawmen who strove to make this part of Arizona safe for settlement.

One of the strangest women to reside in Nogales at the turn of the century was Teresa Urrea, known both as the Saint of Cabora and the Witch of Nogales. Teresa's poor Native American admirers worshiped her and believed she had curative powers, while others described her as untidy with a bitter animosity toward the Mexican government. Born October 15, 1873, on Rancho Cabora in Sinaloa, Mexico, Teresa was the illegitimate daughter of a Yaqui woman, Cayetana

Santa Teresa Urrea, a resident of Tucson, was considered both a saint and a witch. (Courtesy Arizona Historical Society.)

Chavez, and a wealthy rancher, Tomás Urrea. In 1880, Tomás moved his family, including Teresa and her mother, servants, vaqueros, oxen, horses, and cattle, to Sonora. Teresa, a tall beautiful girl with dark brown hair and large luminous eyes, studied herbs with María, a *curandera* ("curer") and accompanied her on visits to the sick. María noticed that Teresa exerted a strong curative influence on the sick.

In 1889, Teresa sank into a deep coma for a couple of weeks. Upon awakening, she claimed to have been present with the saints and the Virgin Mary, who had instructed her to help people. Her earliest miracle involved a *vaquero* whose arm and leg had been paralyzed when a burro kicked him in the head. When Teresa mixed her saliva with soil and rubbed the poultice on his limbs, he immediately rose and used his arm. As her fame as a miracle worker spread, hosts of sick people arrived at Cabora. Teresa refused their money, but her father charged a nominal cost for food to those who could afford it.

The Mexican government feared Teresa and the Catholic church sought to discredit her, but the humble masses of people paid no attention to the priests who railed against her from the pulpit. In 1892, the Mayo tribe seized the town of Navajoa and waylaid Federal troops while they shouted, "Long live Teresa the queen of the Mayos and Yaquis, the saint of Cabora." Federal troops held Teresa and Tomás under house arrest in Guaymas for several days before putting the Urreas onto a heavily guarded train destined for Nogales and ordering the household never to return to Mexico.

The citizens of Nogales turned out in large numbers to welcome Teresa. Tomás moved his household several miles north of town near Calabasas where the sick and crippled, as well as political refugees from both sides of the border, found them. On August 12, 1896, Yaquis shouting, "Viva Santa Teresa," charged across the border and captured the Nogales customs house. Mexican authorities insisted that Teresa had encouraged the attack, but she denied any participation in these uprisings. Before the day ended, seven Yaquis, each carrying a newsprint photograph of Teresa, were dead.

When the Mexican government urged American authorities to remove Teresa farther away from the border, Tomás moved his household to Clifton, Arizona. Here, Teresa continued to perform miracles and went on a tour for a bogus pharmaceutical company in New York. When she learned that her father had died of typhoid fever, she returned to Arizona. A Clifton doctor discovered that she had tuberculosis, but she refused to let him tell her family. On January 11, 1906, Teresa Urrea died at age 33.

During this decade, Nogales obtained clear title to 1 square mile of property in 1896 and subsequently petitioned the U.S. government for a patent. Two years later, in December, Nogales received a patent signed by President William McKinley. In October of 1919, Nogales, with a population of 3,000, was officially proclaimed a city. Nogales was the fifth largest town in the Arizona Territory and the largest city on the border. Mayor William F. Overton held the patented land in trust for the residents, who became property owners upon payment of $5 for their lot plus $7 for execution of the deed.

Santa Cruz, after a four-year fight, became a county with Nogales as the county seat. Advocates for independent government resented having to pay $10.30 for a round trip to Tucson when they had to serve as jurors or participate in other county business. In March 1895, Harry Chenoweth introduced a bill to create a new county known as Grant, but the territorial legislature took no action. Four years later, F.A. Stevens, a Pima County representative, supported by a Nogales delegation led by George Marsh, proposed creating Papago County, but this bill was also defeated. During the spring session, Stevens tried again and on March 15, 1899, the Territorial Assembly and Governor Nathan Oakes Murphy signed the bill creating Santa Cruz County. The House voted unanimously to create the new county and the Council (Senate) voted 7-5 in favor. Those voting "yea" included J.H. Carpenter, Morris Goldwater, George W.P. Hunt, J.M. Murphy, D.K. Udall, George A. Wolff, and A.C. Wright. In the future, the Udalls and the Goldwaters would find themselves on opposite sides of the political fence. Santa Cruz County's first board of supervisors consisted of Rollen Rice Richardson, George Atkinson, and Adolphus H. Noon.

When the news broke about Santa Cruz County's creation, a man ran out into the street waving the telegram. A fire bell went off, whistles blew, and all manner

The 1907 Santa Cruz County Medical Society included, from left to right, (front row) Dr. William L. Chenoweth, Dr. John L. Nickolson, and Dr. Juan Lopez; (back row) Dr. A.L. Gustetter, Dr. Adolphus Noon, and Dr. H.W. Purdy.

of arms were fired off. People in the Nogales "suburbs" thought the Yaquis had invaded the city again, and strangers in hotels and saloons dove under tables. Governor Murphy appointed Colonel Willis P. Harlow as district attorney and William Barnett as sheriff. On March 25, the Santa Cruz board of supervisors leased 12 rooms at $100 a month from George B. Marsh to be used as offices and a jail. Ed Williams filed the first two court cases over promissory notes and won by default.

On the first day of court, which was held in the theater, Frank Duffy was admitted to the bar. On January 5, 1902, Congress authorized Santa Cruz County to issue bonds in the amount of $35,000 to build a courthouse and a jail. The board of supervisors purchased a lot on the corner of Morley Avenue and Court Street from Anton Proto for $2,000. Roy & Titcomb, using architect James Vandevort's drawings, built a combination courthouse and jail of rough native limestone blocks for $28,200. The Pauley Jail Building Company of St. Louis, Missouri installed a four-cell jail, and F.F. Rodrigues installed the courthouse water system. This two-story building, now a museum, features a dome topped with the figure Astraea, Goddess of Justice.

When the new Santa Cruz County Board of Supervisors and the Pima County Board of Supervisors met to distribute the property and funds, Pima County came "loaded for bear," but Santa Cruz arrived in a "very friendly spirit." Pima County tried to get Santa Cruz County to pay for its courthouse improvement and accept part of the financial burden for the fraudulent, defunct Narrow Gauge Railroad. The *Oasis* reported that this was a "huge joke too humorous for words."

Building of the old Santa Cruz County Courthouse, now a museum, was authorized in 1902. The dome is topped with Astrea, the Goddess of Justice. (Courtesy Mary Bingham.)

Sheriff William H. Barnett's first administration was short lived. On May 12, 1899, he and Supervisor George Atkinson tendered their resignations. Evidently there had been political problems because Barnett told the board of supervisors, "this is what you have been sparring for ever since I was appointed." Barnett died of heart trouble on March 26, 1923 at age 64 at his Patagonia home. His successor Thomas F. Brodrick held a number of offices, including town marshal, deputy sheriff, sheriff, constable, and deputy U.S. marshal. Brodrick told Arizona promoter George Hilzinger that "except for an occasional drunk, time would hang so heavily on his hands, that he would be compelled to run for some more offices." He believed that he had the right to expect more occupation and suggested importing a few desperadoes from the East to give some of our peace officers some decent entertainment.

Obviously, Brodrick's propaganda was delivered to attract settlers and eastern business investments because he had his hands full with law enforcement. In 1899, during a preliminary hearing before Judge Harrison at Lochiel, the district attorney appeared on behalf of the Arizona Territory and Frank Duffy served as counsel for M.H. Jones, a salesman from Duquesne, accused of shooting and killing a friend without provocation. Brodrick had captured and jailed Jones. After the hearing, Jones was judged insane and Sheriff Brodrick transferred him to the territorial asylum in Phoenix. Newspapers reasoned that because Jones had patented a railroad case, "it was thought that the concentration of his mind on one subject may have thrown him off balance."

On September 16, the cowboy Domingo Bueno, while looking for a horse belonging to Nogales druggist Charles Cassanova, found a body hanging from a scrub oak in the Pajarito Mountains. He got Sheriff Brodrick and Judge Lee Mix, and guided them to the spot of the heinous crime by lantern light. Brodrick empaneled a coroner's jury and determined that the man, with bullet holes in his skull, had been shot and then hanged to make it look like a suicide. Brodrick formed a posse, but the murderer was never found, nor was the identity of the victim determined.

Many Nogales businessmen combined business and politics. William Schuckmann, born in Hesse, Germany on November 24, 1862, emigrated to America at age 25 and traveled to Wisconsin, where he farmed and clerked in a hardware store. In 1889, he accepted a job as an assayer and superintendent of the Grand Central Mine Company in Sonora, Mexico. In 1894, he returned to Milwaukee and spent three years as an employee of the Gettleman Brewing Company. He married Ms. L. Gettleman before returning to Nogales. Schuckmann worked as a cigar manufacturer until 1915 when he was appointed cashier at the Santa Cruz Valley and Trust Company. That same year, President Woodrow Wilson appointed him postmaster of Nogales. Schuckmann served two terms as city councilman, one term on the Santa Cruz County board of supervisors, and as a director for the Nogales board of trade.

In 1898, the Montezuma Hotel installed an electric clock in the lobby and a female public stenographer set her business downtown. A 20-mile telephone

Longtime Nogales judge Frank J. Duffy was admitted to the bar on the first day of court in Nogales. (Courtesy Arizona Department of Library, Archives and Public Records.)

line was strung between Washington Camp and Nogales and the speakers' voices could be heard "very clearly." A curfew bell warned youngsters to get home and a schoolyard fence separated girls and boys. In November, many Nogales men watched the Corbett-Fitzsimmons fight on Veriscope, an early movie projector. Julian Saboteur, a native of France, opened a fashionable store at the corner of Morley and International that he called La Ville de Paris.

Nogales's early attempts at banking and keeping people's money safe were very successful. The First National Bank of Nogales, established on January 3, 1903, took its place in the financial circles and contributed to the commercial and industrial progress of the Line city. The bank, which conducted a safe conservative policy, was owned by its president, Bracey Curtis, and a number of associates who had established the Sandoval National Bank of Nogales, Arizona, with a capital stock of $25,000. On December 16, the comptroller of the currency authorized the name to be changed from the Sandoval National Bank of Nogales to The First National Bank and. on February 20, 1905, the owners authorized an increase in capital stock from $25,000 to $50,000. In 1905, the surplus and undivided profits of the bank were $65,000. Bank officers included the cashier Otto Herold, Grover Marsteller, town clerk, Theodore Gebler, vice president, and assistant cashier Theron Richardson.

The First National Bank of Nogales served as the depository of public funds not only for Santa Cruz County and Nogales, but for the United States when the post office, the immigration office, and custom house funds were deposited in its vaults. Payments for federal and local government were handled in the First National. The *Oasis* of December 25, 1912, reported the following:

> The First National Bank of Nogales is one which might be emulated with profit by many far more pretentious. When the panic of 1907 struck Arizona it was almost the only financial institution in the state which met all of its obligations without hesitation or reservation and paid all checks presented at its counter without giving out to depositors the admonition to draw lightly, nor did it limit the amounts drawn to small sums, as was the case with banks in Phoenix, Bisbee, Tucson, Douglas and other places; and, for that matter, all over the United States.

A fire on June 9, 1904 destroyed the Nogales railroad depot, the local Wells Fargo office, the Western Union office, and several freight cars. Firemen bravely fought to save the town. In 1906, the Nogales city council made plans for a new city hall, leased a site for a city reservoir, and purchased a wagon and mule for street cleaning. A committee oversaw the construction of a bandstand in the park, and Walter Neumann opened a movie theater and a roller skating rink on Nelson Avenue. Camp Stephen Little, which would become an integral part of the economic, military, and social fabric of the community, was established in Nogales in November of 1910 with a detachment of U.S. Infantry soldiers from Fort Huachuca.

All of Santa Cruz County actively participated in the Statehood Convention in Phoenix to support Arizona's application for statehood status, insisting the Arizona Territory had proved itself capable of responsible government. Democrats and Republicans united to denounce the proposition of admitting Arizona and New Mexico as a single state. Easterners feared that the admission of two states might give Arizona and New Mexico a disproportionate influence in congress.

Responsible government meant good law enforcement in controlling the criminal element on both sides of the border. A curious newspaper tribute to a murderer on June 6, 1908 gives us some insight into the values of the times and the conditions under which lawmen operated:

> Last Saturday at Guaymas, Doroteo Majia, better known in Nogales and throughout the State of Sonora as Tello was shot and instantly killed by Margarito Ayala a Commission Agent, with whom he had a quarrel while drunk. About twenty years ago, Tello, who was a gambler by

profession, shot and instantly killed Hank Frost a Nogales Peace Officer, who had killed Tello's friend. Several years ago Tello killed an officer of the Mexican Army at Hermosillo with whom he had trouble over a woman. With all his faults, Tello was better than many men, and his word was better than most men's bond.

In 1901, Arizona Governor Nathan Oakes formed a mounted company of lawmen, the Arizona Rangers, to bring law and order to the border and to stamp out cattle rustling. The Arizona Rangers were not always appreciated by local law enforcement authorities, who claimed that the Rangers interfered more than they helped. Jefferson "Jeff" Kidder, who spent most of his ranger service in Nogales, rode the border, hounding smugglers, outlaws, cattle rustlers, and gun runners. The *Vidette* described Kidder as a level-headed officer and a gentleman, but his enemies viewed him as arrogant and a good pistoleer. When undesireables threatened Nogales's peace and quiet, Kidder ran them out of town. He was murdered in Naco, Sonora when a prostitute, who had set him up, screamed for the police. The police barged in and shot Kidder, who lived for a few days and died at age 33.

In 1902, Santa Cruz County elected Tom Turner as sheriff. Turner, born on February 5, 1860 in Leon County, Texas, settled on an Arizona ranch along the San Pedro River near Benson and invested in a few head of cattle. One night

This photo of a 1904 Southern Pacific railroad station was taken the same year a fire destroyed the Nogales railroad depot, a Wells Fargo office, and the Western Union office. (Courtesy Pimería Alta Historical Society.)

Early Santa Cruz County sheriff Tom Turner was fined $14 for drinks for shooting three rustlers who stole 26 of his horses. (Courtesy Pimería Alta Historical Society.)

when a band of four Mexican rustlers ran off with 26 of his horses, Turner trailed the men to the Chiricahua Mountains where he shot and killed three of the outlaws, but the fourth got away. For his trouble, Turner got a bullet in his leg. He turned himself in to the Willcox justice of the peace, who took him to breakfast. A coroner's jury convened, held an inquest, and the bodies were returned to Willcox for burial. The party then retired to a saloon where the judge addressed Turner with stern words: "Young man, you have committed a very serious offense and you deserve the severest punishment this court can inflict on you. Damned if I don't fine you drinks for the town for letting the other rustler get away." Turner rousted up all the Willcox males and it cost him $14.

During a roundup, some well-lubricated cowboys decided to ride their horses into a dance at the Nogales Masonic Hall, but the horses objected to climbing the steps. The cowboys felt cheated of their fun and shot out the street lights. The next day, Turner gave them a scorching lecture:

You were just out for a good time and did not mean any harm, but I am the sheriff for the boys in town as well as you and I am not supposed to let things like that happen. I warn you don't do it anymore or I will have to come and get you.

Washington Camp desperately needed its new sub-jail. Early mining communities usually dumped their prisoners in abandoned mine tunnels, but the one at Washington Camp had become too congested and resembled the "Black Hole of Calcutta." On March 15, Sheriff Turner and Deputy Durnal were about to ride out to Washington Camp to inspect prisoners who were working on the Lochiel-Duquesne road, when a young boy ran up and said a woman was being killed near the Nogales cemetery. The lawmen found Andres Espiridion venting his wrath on Dionicia Mavante, a Yaqui woman with whom he lived from time to time. When Espiridion assaulted the sheriff, Turner fired on him. The sheriff's horse spooked, so he dismounted and fired again. In a few minutes, Espiridion was "cooled down by death," but the dead woman's head was beaten into an unrecognizable mass. Turner and Durnal loaded the bodies onto a wagon and took them to Nogales. The sheriff and the deputy were complimented for their bravery and prompt action.

On December 16, 1902, the jail doors slammed shut on cattle rustler Fernando Valenzuela at Washington Camp after a 10-mile running battle during which more than 25 shots were fired. After Dan Sheehy brought down Valenzuela's horse, the bandit barricaded himself behind the animal and shot off half of Sheehy's hat. Sheehy caught and tied up Valenzuela before delivering him to the jail. A petition was circulated to make Sheehy a deputy.

On January 15, Jerry Sheehy shot and killed Richard W. Harrison at a roundup in the San Rafael Valley. Witnesses testified that Harrison accused Sheehy of "throwing his place out for settlement" and calling him a "son-of-a-bitch." Sheehy and Harrison faced each other on horseback with their bridles in their left hands. Harrison threw a punch at Sheehy, who ducked. He struck again and connected. The men scuffled for a few minutes, separated, and then Sheehy drew his pistol and fired at Harrison. Sheehy rode off, turned, and fired again. Harrison fell and when the cowboys gathered around the corpse, Sheehy said, "C'mon boys, let's get these cattle away."

When Sheriff Turner took Sheehy into the Nogales jail, Harrison's friends formed a lynch mob. Turner stood off the mob and insisted that he would not turn his prisoner over to anyone. The trial was moved to Tucson where Sheehy was convicted of manslaughter and sentenced to nine years in the territorial prison. Jerry Sheehy was pardoned in 1908 and died in Tucson at age 88. Turner's successor, Sheriff Charles Fowler's grandson, still lives in Nogales and teaches history at Elderhostel classes.

On January 28, 1905, Nogales newspapers carried banner headlines: "Terrible Tragedy—Lives of Four Men Blighted out in as Many Minutes." M.M. Conn had hired gambler Ferdinand Walters, a.k.a. the Catalina Kid, to run a poker game in his Palace Saloon. When patrons accused Walters of using marked cards, George Howards, a Palace employee, told Walters there would be no crookedness and asked him to turn the game over to William Abel. Walters casually remarked there would be a few dead men before sunrise and left. A while later, he returned to the Palace in his red satin-lined cape and ordered dinner. After his meal, he went to the bar where J.J. "Cowboy" Johnson was talking to Charles Casteel. Walters drew a .45 Colt and fired at Johnson from about 4 feet. He then fired at Conn and at George Spindle, who was sitting next to Modesto Olivas. The last bullet passed through Spindle's hat rim and struck Olivas in the head. Walters stepped over Conn, walked out into the street and fired a fourth shot into his own head. Jess Marleau went for Sheriff Fowler and said, "They just had a little shooting scrape down at Conn's saloon." "Anybody hurt?" asked Fowler. "Only four" was the reply. Rumors circulated that Dave Black, a hired gunman, had followed Walters outside and shot him, but Dave would never say. In 1908, the court judged Dave Black insane and, on January 18, Sheriff Harry Saxon took him to the territorial insane asylum in Phoenix. The *Vidette* wrote, "A more generous, warm hearted man never lived than Dave Black. Black was an admirer of President

Early Santa Cruz County sheriff Charles Fowler succeeded Tom Turner. (Courtesy Pimería Alta Historical Society.)

(Theodore) Roosevelt, and imagined his friend the president was going to send him $1,000."

Harry Saxon took office as sheriff at age 24 in 1907, the year that saw the end of gambling in Arizona. In Nogales, the Palace, the Monte Carlo, and other gambling houses closed down at midnight on March 31. Saxon, born on July 24, 1882 in the San Gabriel Valley, held several offices in Santa Cruz County, including mounted customs inspector, sheriff, Santa Cruz cattle inspector, chairman of the livestock sanitary board, investigator for the Mexican government under President Alvaro Obregón, president of the Sulphur Springs Valley chamber of commerce, president of the Arizona Cattle Growers' Association, and mayor of Willcox. He died at the age of 82 in Tucson on August 11, 1962.

Ambos Nogales continued to have cooperative relations and Americans and Mexicans traveled freely back and forth across the border. Morgan Wise, the American Consul in Nogales, Sonora, kept matters running smoothly not only between the two cities, but between the two countries. Morgan, while on his

Morgan Wise, appointed American consul in Nogales Sonora by President Grover Cleveland, maintained cooperative relations on both sides of the border.

way to California in 1850, stopped to pan for gold on the Feather River. He returned to Pennsylvania where he resumed his education and graduated from Waynesburg College. Morgan, prominent in democratic politics, served for two terms each as Pennsylvania state senator and as representative to Congress from the 21st Pennsylvania District. In 1882, President Grover Cleveland appointed him American consul in Nogales, Sonora, Mexico. When his term expired, he engaged in ranching and mining at Calabasas until his death in 1902. His widow Catherine lived to a ripe old age and made her home in Nogales with her son Joseph E. Wise.

Their son Joseph was born in Waynesburg, Pennsylvania on February 21, 1867. He arrived in Nogales a year after his parents and engaged in the cattle business near Calabasas. He also served as an organizer and a director of the Santa Cruz Valley Bank and Trust Company. In the 1914 settlement of the Baca Float Grant No. 3, the U.S. Supreme Court decreed to Joseph Wise title to 1,000 acres of land. The federal court at Tucson also decreed to him and his sister title to one-nineteenth of the entire Baca Float, his share consisting of more than 5,000 acres, making Joseph Wise one of the wealthiest ranchers in Santa Cruz County.

Nogales proudly celebrated the 1908 Fourth of July in grand style. The gala began in the morning with a horse race on Grand Avenue. Afterwards, people watched a baseball game, a wild west show, a bucking horse contest, and enjoyed a free barbecue. Jack Dunn and Bob Daley from Patagonia won a $350 prize in the double-handed hard rock drilling contest when they drilled through 33 inches of hard granite in record time. That night, a parade and torchlight procession led by the Nogales Fire Department and the Nogales Brass Band in sparkling white uniforms stopped in front of the Montezuma Hotel, where Territorial Governor George Kibbey made a rousing speech at the reception before the grand ball.

The automobile changed Nogales as it did the rest of the nation. Local attorney Walter McCurdy bought a 1902 automobile, the first in town, and treated his friends to "runs about town at a rapid clip." Harry Karns was arrested in 1908 for driving his new automobile at an unheard-of speed of 6 miles per hour within the town limits. His court hearing attracted a huge crowd. Karns admitted his guilt and the judge fined him $10. Karns, a structural engineer, designed the Nogales water works and served three terms as mayor. In his later years, he became an authority on early Spanish exploration in the Nogales area.

Life was getting interesting south of the border and Nogales looked nervously over its shoulder as there came rumblings of a revolution in Mexico.

9. War on the Border and Abroad

During this decade, Arizona celebrated the achievement of statehood on February 14, 1912. During Prohibition, the thirsty flocked south of the border to wet their whistles. Bullets of the revolution sprayed across the border when the Sonorans put up their candidate for president, Alvaro Obregón, and now there were rumors of war abroad. The U.S. Infantry camp, with white officers and black enlisted men near Morley and Hudgin Streets, grew larger to protect Americans in case of an "accident."

Newspapers had a wonderful time with the Mexican Revolution and reporters such as Hanson Ray Sisk, born in Kentucky on July 15, 1892, came to Nogales in 1914 to cover it and stayed to become a part of Nogales. Sisk purchased the *Nogales Herald* in 1918 from Judge R.L. O'Neal. He served as president of the Arizona Newspaper Association and vice president of the Nogales chamber of commerce. In 1921, Craig Pottinger, who went on to publish the *Nogales International*, recalled that Sisk hired him because his last editor had such a bad case of delirium tremens that he jumped through a hospital window. Sisk's death from a heart attack on October 23, 1969 shocked the Nogales community. He was laid to rest holding the October 21 edition of the *Herald* in which his last column of "Views and Interviews" appeared.

Not only bullets caused consternation for Ambos Nogales. Hordes of Chinese, victims of increasing racism, fled Mexico when Mexicans found themselves out of work and resentful of Chinese financial success. Fear of a Chinese invasion on the American side of the border led to the passage of the Chinese Exclusion Act, which was not repealed until 1943, a law that provided for the rejection of Chinese laborers, skilled and unskilled, and those engaged in mining.

The Chinese Six Corporation, with offices in Shanghai and San Francisco, brought in illegal Chinese aliens and engaged in the smuggling of opium. If a Chinese man who was already in the country could pay to bring in a friend or relative, he contacted the local Chinese Six representative. The agent passed on this information to the Shanghai office, which found the prospective newcomer and notified him to go to Shanghai.

Once the alien had received his preliminary instructions in English and in American manners in China, arrangements would be made to have him travel by ship to Mexico where he would be met by a Six company agent. This agent would see to it that the alien got work in a restaurant or laundry where he would become used to his new life. Finally, he would be sent by train to Nogales, Sonora and turned over to a Mexican who would deliver him to an American town across the border such as Nogales, Naco, or Agua Prieta, Arizona or Mexicali, California. When he first arrived in the United States, he would memorize a complete description of his home in China, along with fictional names of parents, siblings, the school he attended, and playmates. The 1906 San Francisco earthquake destroyed most records and, from that time, Chinese aliens claimed to have been born there, well aware that no one could prove them wrong. Aliens were expected to pay the Six company for their expenses and those who did not were assassinated by a company hatchet man.

If an alien came before a deportation hearing, the Six company arranged for delays while the accused received additional instruction and clothes. Very soon,

Hanson Ray Sisk, early Nogales newspaper publisher, came to Nogales to cover the Mexican Revolution, only to remain and purchase the Nogales Herald. *(Courtesy Pimería Alta Historical Society.)*

homesick Chinese learned that if they wanted to go home, they had only to get in a fight, go to jail, and get deported, and they would get a free ride home to China. Santa Cruz County Sheriff Harry Saxon often found his jail overflowing with Chinese who wanted nothing more than to go home.

When the fighting between the rebel groups got serious on the border, the accident so many had feared happened on November 26, 1915. Private Stephen D. Little was killed in action on Crawford Street Hill during an all-day battle in Nogales, Sonora with bullets and refugees spilling over the border. Mayor Lee W. Mix saw the city through these difficult times. Mix, born in Batavia, New York on April 19, 1849, as a child moved with his parents to Cleveland, Ohio then to Wheeling, West Virginia. Mix began his career at the early age of 14 when he learned his father's drugstore business. After a brief period in Memphis, Tennessee, he moved to San Francisco in 1875, where he worked as a stockbroker and became associated with William T. Coleman, president of the Citizens' Safety Committee. A year later, he joined the California National Guard and succeeded C.F. Crocker as second lieutenant of Company G of the 2nd Artillery.

In 1880, Mix joined Malter Lind and Company, engineers and contractors for mining machinery in Tombstone, Arizona and Sonora, Mexico. He took up legal residence in Nogales in 1885 and developed the St. Helena mine, which he ultimately sold to an English company. Mix served as president of the Nogales Light, Ice and Water Company and vice president and director of Roy & Titcomb. Mix and his wife Dolores Escalante of Hermosillo had five children. He served

This early U.S.–Mexico garita, *or guardhouse, on Morley Avenue appeared in the early 1920s. Customs officials checked people and merchandise crossing the border.*

This Mexican Revolution photo was probably taken after the 1913 Battle of Nogales. It shows the execution of a man accused of being a traitor and refusing to accept the winning regime.

on Nogales's first school board, as the chief of the first volunteer fire department, and was elected mayor of Nogales in 1912 and 1914 on the citizen's ticket.

As a result of the Volstead Act, on December 31, 1914, every saloon in Arizona went dry. Nogales, Sonora boomed with bootleggers and soon there were so many that they had to wear badges to keep from buying from each other. Visitors sending home postcards clearly delineated which side of "the Line" was wet and which was dry. The Donnadieu brothers opened a large cave as a speakeasy and heated and lit it with gas. Thus La Caverna Restaurant, which in later years was an elegant tourist attraction until it burned down in the 1970s, had a humble start. Priscu Mercado Navarette recalled many of the names of the bars in Nogales, Sonora and their owners, including the Cantina, the Concordia Club, the Cosmopolitan, El Jacvalito bar, the La Paloma, the White Front, El Cristal, La Gruta, El 14 Bar, the OK Bar, and the Bar and Casa de Juegos Casino, all clustered on one city block. Navarrete knew these bars well because he had a drink in every one. Bullfights across the border provided another diversion.

In an attempt to heal deteriorating conditions between Mexico and the United States, President Woodrow Wilson submitted the U.S. attack on Vera Cruz to a mediation board. This was an attempt to find a peaceful solution to the revolution, with generals from the southern Mexico warring factions meeting with General John J. "Blackjack" Pershing in Nogales, Arizona. General Pancho Villa and his troops arrived from the east and General Alvaro Obregón traveled by train in Nogales on August 29, 1914, along with Venustiano Carranza and Sonora's Governor José María Maytorena. Villa's military band presented a

La Caverna, or The Caverns, became a very elegant restaurant in Nogales, Sonora, but it started in the 1920s as a speakeasy during Prohibition.

concert in Nogales. Villa, whose 50 personal bodyguards saw to his safety, proudly exhibited two new black cars in his entourage. Villa and his staff ate breakfast at the Montezuma. Later in the day, the generals were entertained by General Pershing's 12th U.S. Infantry band.

On November 19, 1914, Nogales dignitaries laid a cornerstone for the new Town Hall. City officials moved into their new offices on February 14, 1915. The year 1914 saw raging floods along the Santa Cruz and Walter Fortune, a member of the Santa Cruz County Board of Supervisors, drowned near Harshaw Creek. His body was not found for over a year and his remains were identified by his boots. A bridge was built over the Santa Cruz River, a larger electric light, power, and ice plant was constructed, and a $150,000 bond issue for county road improvement was approved by the voters. Theodora Marsh, widow of merchant George Marsh, who sat on the power plant's board of directors, also served as an officer of the Santa Cruz Valley Bank, operated the National Hotel, and in 1916, was elected to the state legislature. When T.B. Dillon and his wife visited Nogales, they arrived with as many as 50 burros loaded with high-grade ore, which they sold to assayer Hugo Miller for top price. Duquesne and Washington Camp employed 400 miners, and a new tramway and concentrator were being built at the Flux.

Mayor Mix sent out letters to the mayors of all Arizona cities and towns, urging them to join in a petition to Congress to have the largest dreadnought then being built for the United States named the USS *Arizona*. The petition was successful and, as a result, Arizona Senators Marcus A. Smith and Henry F. Ashurst and

Pancho Villa was one of the most colorful generals of the Mexican Revolution. (Courtesy Special Collections, University of Arizona Library.)

Representative Carl Hayden telegraphed the Arizona newspapers on July 10 that the Secretary of the Navy had announced the vessel would be named for the state of Arizona. In 1915, Arizona Governor George W.P. Hunt appointed a state committee chaired by Mayor Mix to arrange for the launching ceremonies of the battleship USS *Arizona*. The White House and Secretary of the Navy received a special contingent of Arizona representatives in Washington, D.C. and on July 19, the launching ceremonies of the largest battleship ever built in the United States took place at the New York Navy Yard. The *Arizona*, which never fired her guns in anger, was destroyed during Japan's bombing of Pearl Harbor.

In 1915, the voters elected Lucretia Roberts Constable of Canelo and she was appointed a deputy sheriff of Santa Cruz County. When she spoke to a group of women in New York, she wore her badge and six-shooters. Years later, her son Richard wrote a novel, *Star in the West*, which was made into a movie starring Debbie Reynolds and Andy Griffin. Lucretia married Nogales barber George Januel.

When school started in September 1915, three teachers taught 145 students in Patagonia. In Nogales, only 600 children could be accommodated and more than 100, those with alien parents, had to be turned away. The first Santa Cruz County Fair was held in October of that year on 10 acres donated by rancher Wade Purdum. First prize for draft stallions went to the Elgin Percheron Breeder's Association. Oliver J. Rothrock received a first place ribbon for his three-gaited saddle horse and Laura Parsons won her blue ribbon for her embroidered shirt. The highlight was a race between four Model-T Fords. A month later, H.M.

After the Battle of Nogales, Sonora on March 13, 1913, people watched as the dead were carted off the battlefield. One victim fell off the wagon.

Clagett and Louis Hudgin, owners of the Nogales Jersey Farm, returned from the state fair in Phoenix with a sweepstakes prize for their dairy cows.

Upheavals along the border continued with Pancho Villa's attack on Columbus, New Mexico, during the early morning hours on March 9, 1916. Continuing border raids convinced the U.S. Army that Pancho Villa had to go and that additional troops were required to protect border communities. Pershing launched his famous offensive into Mexico and President Woodrow Wilson mobilized 160,000 national guardsmen, who bivouacked along the border.

With the assassination of Mexico's President Francisco Madero and the refusal of Sonorans to accept Victoriano Huerta, the state of Sonora and Ambos Nogales became focal points of the revolution. Arizona "hardware stores" did a brisk business supplying arms to all factions of the war. On May 17, 1913, Nogales Town Marshal J.K. Wright, Nogales Sonora Prefect A.C. Villaseñor, and the Montezuma bartender Jack Williams were brought to trial for violation of the U.S. neutrality law. Lieutenant John Milikin of the 5th Regiment of Cavalry swore out complaints before U.S. Commissioner Allen T. Bird. The men were found guilty of attempted bribery and stealing U.S. government arms and ammunition and selling it to rebel forces.

Sonoran rebels attacked Nogales, Sonora, which was guarded by 400 crack troops under Colonels Bernardo Reyes and General Emilio Kosterlitzky. During the Battle of Nogales on March 13, 1913, sightseers, packing picnic baskets from all over Arizona, could not be driven away by spraying bullets. Ada EKey Jones watched the battle through binoculars from her home on a hill. Captain Cornelius C. Smith, Commander of G Troop, 5th U.S. Cavalry, had anticipated the battle and reasoned that American lives and property would be in danger.

In the time leading up to the battle, Kosterlitzky, who knew that his insufficient Mexican federal forces were in grave danger, stationed his 285 men on the hills commanding the approaches to Nogales. When Captain Smith dined with him, Kosterlitzky said the following:

> Obregón is on his way here with about 2,500 men. I will fight him, of course, but am at a disadvantage with less than three hundred rurales and a few regular troops under Lieutenant Colonel Manuel Reyes. If I have to surrender, I will cross the line and surrender to you.

They agreed that American soldiers would remain on the international line and would not fire unless fired upon. Smith sent out patrols along the U.S. side of the border and ordered the streets of Nogales, Arizona, cleared. On March 12, additional American troops under the command of Lieutenant Colonel Daniel Tate arrived from Fort Huachuca. The battle began at daybreak the next day, and bullets peppered buildings and houses. They hit several Americans, including Private Allen A. Umfleet of G Troop, Hilario Perez, a child playing in his yard, Leopoldo Nuñez, and Pablo Rubio. Mrs. H.W. Kelsey was understandably distraught when a bullet whizzed between her legs through her skirt while she

Colonel Emilio Kosterlitzky poses with his family. Kosterlitzky, head of Mexico's federal forces, led the troops guarding Nogales, Sonora in 1913. (Courtesy Pimería Alta Historical Society.)

was hanging up laundry. Her husband later extracted the bullet from their porch. Several American homes were hit, including those of Sheriff McKnight, W.A. Edwards, William Schuckman, and Fred Von Mourick.

William S. McKnight and Deputy Sheriff Frank Taylor openly declared themselves against the Mexican rebels. McKnight, who had been elected Santa Cruz County sheriff on the Republican ticket in 1911, was born in Illinois on October 12, 1864. He arrived in Arizona on April 12, 1887, operated the Humboldt gold and silver mine and the Arivaca mine, and helped erect the Old Glory Stamp Mill. McKnight also worked as a ranch foreman for Rollin Rice Richardson at Patagonia and as butcher in Nogales. After serving as sheriff, he was appointed beef inspector and at the end of this term, he received the government contract to furnish beef to Camp Little and Fort Huachuca. He married Geneva Crocomb, a native of California, and they had nine children.

The bullet that hit Private Umfleet passed through his neck and up though his mouth and exited through his nose. Miraculously, he recovered and soon returned to duty. American Colonel Tate ordered the Mexican combatants to a cease-fire and, with a good position on Crawford Hill, he threatened to open fire on them if they did not obey. The bugler sounded the Mexican retreat and Kosterlitzky and his men came down out of the hills under a flag of truce, gathered at the Customs house, crossed Bonillas Bridge, and stacked their arms along Calle International in Nogales, Arizona. Kosterlitzky told J.B. Mix, the U.S. Customs Official, "Well Jim, it's all up. We have done our best but we will have to give up." Kosterlitzky wrote, "My forces had four men killed, five wounded and five taken prisoner." Obregón reported, "I lost six dead and nine wounded." Albert Conrad, a Nogales mining man, traveled to Magdalena and brought Kosterlitzky's family to Nogales where they remained for six months.

A demand that the U.S. territory be respected came again on November 26, 1915 at about 10:00 a.m. when Colonel William H. Sage, in command of the U.S. Infantry, ordered his men to return the fire of Villa's soldiers who were evacuating Nogales, Sonora. American soldiers assumed prone positions on International Street, with their guns facing Mexico, ready for action. Sage instructed the soldiers to fire only at those firing on Americans from Mexico, and to avoid shooting noncombatants. When American sharpshooters climbed on building roofs to search for Mexican snipers, gunfire commenced in earnest as bullets knew nothing of borders and international treaties.

During the heaviest fire, the Carranza-Obregón forces, who emerged from the hills surrounding Nogales, did not recognize the American soldiers, and opened fire, killing three and wounding two. The Americans returned gunfire,

Nogales turned out to bid farewell to Private Stephen D. Little, who was killed on November 26, 1915 in Nogales, Arizona during the Mexican Revolution. (Courtesy Pimería Alta Historical Society.)

but as soon as the mistake was discovered, the firing ceased. General Obregón and Colonel Sage met on the international line and extended proper apologies and salutations.

Private Stephen B. Little of I Company, 12th Infantry, from Fairmont, North Carolina, had been killed near the top of the hill on Crawford Street and two more American men were wounded. The Mexican death toll was estimated from 75 to 100. Pancho Villa and his forces, who hated President Woodrow Wilson for not recognizing the Villistas, continued to cast slurs and insults at the President, the United States Army, and Americans in general as they retreated.

The Nogales post was renamed Camp Stephen Little on December 14, 1915 in memory of Private Little. Rows of tents spilled over Mariposa Canyon and into the neighboring hills. The monthly military payroll reached $350,000. Local merchants and ranchers made a good living furnishing the camp with food and supplies.

Nogales, Sonora, like most Mexican towns, simply accepted the winners and changed allegiances to whomever was in power. However, there was always the occasional hold-out who, accused of treason, would stomp out his cigarette and curse his captors before dropping from the bullets of an execution squad.

In 1917, Nogales, Arizona laid out the red carpet for the revolutionary Generals Pancho Villa and Venustiano Carranza, who were entertained by the officers of the 12th Infantry and their Commander-in-Chief General Pershing, accompanied

General Alvaro Obregón, General Pancho Villa, and General John "Blackjack" Pershing were welcomed to Nogales in 1917. Behind Pershing is a young Dwight D. Eisenhower. (Courtesy Pimería Alta Historical Society.)

Mexican general Benjamín Hill stands with his staff on the outskirts of Nogales, Sonora. After assuming command of Obregón's forces, Hill became a mortal enemy of Pancho Villa.

by a very young Dwight D. Eisenhower. The infantry band gave a concert in the city park and the famous Los Angeles "bird men," a group of young aviators, performed daring feats in their magnificent flying machines.

One of the Mexican generals who frequented Nogales during the revolutionary period was General Benjamín Hill for whom a small town in Sonora is named. A cultured gentleman, as well as a trained military officer educated in Italy, one of his ancestors, another General Benjamin Hill, fought in the United States Civil War. Hill, who fought in the border battles of Naco, Agua Prieta, and Nogales, was eventually caught in the clashes between Generals Pancho Villa and Plutarco Elías-Calles. He became a mortal enemy of Villa when he assumed command of General Alvaro Obregón's forces after a shell shattered Obregón's arm and it had to be amputated. Obregón went crazy with pain and tried to commit suicide.

With smuggling increasing along the border, Congress took steps to create an organization that tracked "man smugglers." In 1917, the first general immigration act was passed and, on May 8, 1924, the United States Border Patrol was created by the Labor Department Appropriations Act. Requirements to join included bachelorhood, along with the ability to ride a horse and shoot. The men provided their own horses. Five years after the creation of the Border Patrol, seven men had died in the line of duty.

When the United States declared war on Europe's central powers on April 6, 1917, the soldiers left Camp Little to fight a war overseas. Now soldiers were needed overseas as well as on the home front. In the autumn of 1917, Nogales

113

Yaquis attempted to invade the United States and were captured by the soldiers of the 10th Cavalry on January 9, 1918. (Courtesy Arizona Historical Society.)

ranchers were worried by reports that renegade Yaqui bands were rustling cattle along the border. Colonel J.C. Frier from Camp Little sent out patrols in the areas around Arivaca, Ruby, Oro Blanco, and eastward toward Lochiel.

On the day of what became known as the Yaqui Incident, Captain Frederick Ryder and E Troop set out along the Oro Blanco trail, which paralleled the border. A local rancher from Ruby, Phil Clarke, had discovered the remains of freshly slaughtered steer along with footprints. In the afternoon, Ryder spied a long column of Native Americans on a ridge. He attempted to chase them, but they disappeared into the rugged terrain. When Ryder and his men dismounted and tried to find the Yaquis in a steep canyon, the Yaquis opened fire. After a brief exchange of gunfire, a Yaqui emerged with hands up and asked for a truce.

Ten Yaquis surrendered, including a 10-year-old boy, but about 20 escaped back over the border. One Yaqui died the next day in a Nogales hospital from his wounds. Ryder tried to turn over his prisoners to Colonel Frier at Camp Little, but the colonel did not want them. Frier put them to work under his command and they turned out to be excellent workers. They told Frier that the only reason they fired on his men was because they thought the African-American troopers were Mexicans whom they would just as soon shoot any time. The nine prisoners were eventually taken to Tucson and indicted for arms smuggling on February 9, 1918. Charges against the boy, Antonio Flores, were dismissed. The Mexican government was having its own troubles and was in no mood to show clemency to its troublemakers. Judge William Sawtelle sentenced the eight men to 30 days in jail after which they were released.

On August 27, 1918, another battle erupted involving Nogales. Lieutenant Colonel Frederick J. Herman, 10th Cavalry, and Lieutenant Robert Scott Israel investigated rumors of Mexicans accompanied by well-dressed Caucasians in and around Ambos Nogales. During the late afternoon, a Mexican tried to cross the border into the United States and ignored the Americans' order to halt. A guard drew his pistol and joined Private W.H. Klint in a chase after the Mexican. Then a Mexican customs guard shot at the Americans and killed Klint. Klint's buddy, Corporal William Tucker, retaliated and shot and killed the customs guard along with three other Mexicans. Americans from both sides of the border joined the melee.

Herman and three troops of the 10th Cavalry proceeded to the border under Captain Roy V. Moreledge, Captain Joseph Hungerford, and Captain H.S.E. Marshburn. Captain Henry C. Carol and his forces were stationed at Titcomb Hill, and Moreledge on Morley Avenue stood poised to enter Mexico should it be necessary. Hungerford and his forces waited near Reservoir Hill. Colonel Herman set up command in the railway depot. Excited Americans ran up and down the streets firing wildly in the direction of Mexico.

As if he did not have enough to do in 1918 with a small jail bursting at the seams with bootleggers and World War I draft dodgers, Herman ordered Raymond R. Earhardt to round up "all well meaning but trigger happy citizens and confine them to the city hall." Earhardt had come to Nogales from Athens, Ohio in 1906 where he worked as a fireman and locomotive engineer on the Ohio railroads. In

These 10th Cavalry African-American soldiers were stationed at Camp Stephen D. Little. (Courtesy Pimería Alta Historical Society.)

115

Arizona, he worked at the Mowry mine as a guard, engineer, and manager before the voters elected him Santa Cruz County sheriff. After he left the sheriff's office, Earhardt served in the state legislature as investigator for the Arizona Industrial Commission and as manager of the Nogales Chamber of Commerce.

The sheriff, assisted by the military, rousted snipers from the Concordia Club. Sergeant Jackson found a group of scantily dressed women huddled in a corner. They chorused, "Sergeant Jackson we are all so glad to see you." An embarrassed Jackson had evidently had occasion to do previous business at the club. An African-American soldier, although sick in the hospital, had no intention of being left out of a good fight. He pulled on his pants, jumped on a horse, hospital gown flapping in the wind, and drew a rifle and ammunition from the armory. Lieutenant Loftus and Corporal Lots of the 35th Infantry were drilled (shot) by snipers. Two Nogales housewives who saw Corporal A.L. Whitworth fall, bravely dragged him to safety.

Shortly after the fight began, Colonel Herman suffered a minor wound in the leg and Captain Carol was wounded in the wrist. Captain Hungerford was shot and killed as he attempted to cross the border. Around 5:45 p.m., Consul E.M. Larson and Sheriff Earhardt delivered a message from the Mexican commander to Colonel Herman saying that if the Americans would run up a white flag and cease firing, the Mexicans would do the same. Herman, who had lost all patience, threatened that if the Mexicans did not stop fighting in 10 minutes, his forces

These men were the first to volunteer for World War I in Nogales. In the right-hand corner is a picture at the Nogales International *where men are reading about the end of the war. (Courtesy Pimería Alta Historical Society.)*

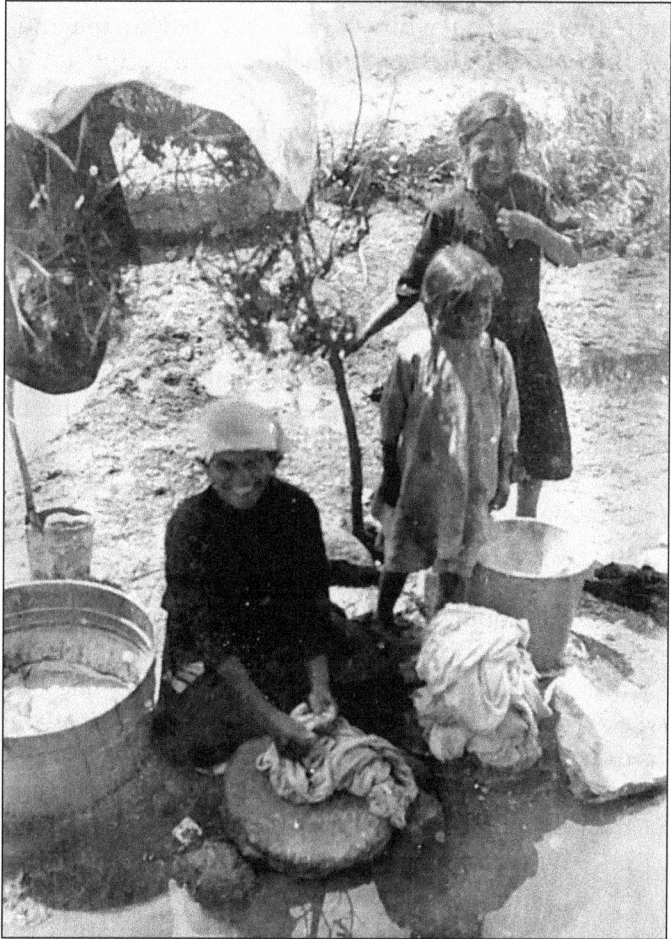

Washerwomen were allowed to accompany the military in the 1920s. This was probably the wife of an enlisted man with their two children.

would burn Nogales, Sonora to the ground. The Mexican commander, seeing that he was outnumbered, ran up the white flag. Around 6:20 p.m., Herman, with Consul Lawton, Lieutenant Robert S. Israel, and a bugler, proceeded to the consulate under heavy guard. The Mexican commander demanded that they surrender their weapons. Herman informed him that he might take them if he could. By now, an American detachment stood assembled in front of the Consulate building and the Mexican leader wisely chose not to pursue the matter.

Total losses on the American side were 2 officers, 3 enlisted men, and several civilians killed, along with 2 officers and 29 men wounded. Later evidence indicated that the sorry affair had been instigated by the Germans, who wanted to preoccupy the United States with Mexico and draw its attention away from Europe. Bodies of German agents provocateur were found and buried with the Mexican dead.

On January 26, 1916, the *International Herald* reported that many applauded and children cried as hooded and masked Ku Klux Klan members carrying torches and, mounted on white horses, paraded to the music of military bands. The Alabama Mystics rode to the Santa Cruz Club for a banquet and dance where everyone wore formal evening dress. The assistant chairman of the reception committee was Colonel William H. Sage, commanding officer.

On April 6, 1917, the United States declared war on Germany and Santa Cruz County responded with fervent patriotism. The Santa Cruz Club, the Nogales Rifle Club, and all able-bodied males formed a home guard and drilled under an army officer. June 5 was declared Registration Day and a legal holiday. "Registered and Ready" buttons were presented to each of the 567 registrants. Women attended workshops and rolled and folded miles of bandages. They also knitted sweaters and the younger women enrolled in a nurse's training school. Nogales oversubscribed its first Liberty Loan drive and the first Nogalians to go to war were presented with a watch by the Santa Cruz Club. That year, the homes in Nogales made certain that every serviceman had a wonderful Christmas dinner. Only about 2,500 men remained at Camp Little, whose halcyon days were a thing of the past.

Being able to cross the border and have drinks with meals made Ambos Nogales a popular convention city during Prohibition. The Elks Club, the Arizona Association of Newspapers, and the State Association of Chambers of Commerce all held conventions in Nogales. The Nogales Rotary Club held its weekly meetings at the Cosmopolitan Grill across the Line. The Ridge Igo post of the American Legion, which organized in Nogales right after the parent group founded in 1919 entertained visiting members at picnic and ball games in a grove near the mayor of Nogales, Sonora's home.

In 1919, members of the chambers of commerce from Ambos Nogales traveled on a special train excursion departing from Nogales, Arizona and visited towns along the west coast of Mexico from February 19 to 26 in an effort to build business connections and repair damage done by the revolution. The journey was dedicated to Mexico's President Venustiano Carranza. Stops were made at the offices of Alvaro Obregón, candidate for Mexico's presidency; Sinaloa Governor Ramón F. Iturbe; and Sonora Governor Plutarco Elías-Calles. Hanson R. Sisk, publisher of the *Nogales Daily Herald*; Colonel Allen T. Bird, editor of the *Daily Morning Oasis*; and A.W. Lohn, the official photographer, accompanied the group. At that time, the United States imported antimony, cattle, copper, lumber, gold, bat guano, graphite, lead, manganese, pearls, garbanzo beans, and silver from Mexico. At stops in each city as far south as Mazatlan, business leaders and politicians were invited to discuss expansion possibilities in both the United States and Mexico.

10. Years of Change: 1920s

During this decade, Nogales dealt with the war on its doorstep and saw its sons go off to fight World War I an ocean away. It managed to find a modicum of normalcy and adopted a charter government. The Nogales Woman's Club organized the town library, the weekly *Nogales International* appeared, and Nogales dedicated its International Airport. A war-weary Mexico saw a brief period of reconciliation between the revolutionary forces, but fighting broke out again in 1929 when Mexico's Six Weeks Revolution erupted, and once again spectators with picnic baskets, along with U.S. troops, amassed on the border.

Ranchers saw a way to supplement their precarious incomes by taking in lodgers, who wanted to be part of the frontier for at least a few weeks and the dude ranch industry grew. After John Burton built a lodge and cottages at the Circle-Z for owners Carl and Lee Zinsmeister, business was so good that the ranch expanded again the next year. Today, the Circle-Z still hosts vacationers anxious to capture the flavor of the Old West.

With financial help from both the United States and Mexico, a wastewater treatment was built to help both cities. Because Nogales, Sonora is higher in elevation than Nogales, Arizona, good sanitary practice dictated that the plant had to be installed for a downgrade. Nogales, Arizona shared water with her sister city to the south during the terrible droughts of 1921 and 1923. Both fire departments fought fires side by side, sometimes scurrying back and forth across the border to take care of more than one fire.

Mexican President Elect Alvaro Obregón visited Nogales and met with Arizona Governor Thomas Campbell. Obregón was also greeted by President Calvin Coolidge's representatives. Hanson Sisk presented the president-elect with a copy of a handbound Nogales *Herald* for the day printed on silk. On January 1, 1928, Obregón had been elected to succeed Calles-Elías as president of Mexico, but less than three weeks later, a young religious fanatic assassinated him in a Mexico City restaurant. Members of the Nogales Chamber of Commerce, who had planned to attend the inauguration, called on Mexican officials with condolences. Emilio Portes Gil was chosen as interim president until new elections could be held.

Harold J. Brown served on the Nogales police force before moving to Pima County in 1919 to serve as a deputy sheriff. Upon his return to Nogales in 1922,

Nogales firemen from both sides of the border helped each other in case of fire. (Courtesy Pimería Alta Historical Society.)

he was elected sheriff. His career also included service as a U.S. deputy marshal, chief field agent for the State Liquor Control Board, yard captain at the State Prison, and inspector for the Motor Vehicle Division. At the outbreak of World War II, Harold J. Brown was sworn into the U.S. Navy as the oldest first-class fireman in the Seabees. He edged in under the 51-year, 6-month maximum age limit by two months. During his tenure as sheriff, Sam Rotge bragged to Brown that he had discovered some of the "finest wild turkey hunting in his whole life. Yes sir." Brown wanted to know where. Rotge obligingly took the sheriff to a spot about 7 miles west of Nogales. It was on Brown's ranch and the turkeys were part of the sheriff's prize flock.

James V. Robins found electioneering could be dangerous. Jimmy was running for Santa Cruz County attorney in 1925 and Deputy Pat Patterson was urging the reelection of Sheriff Harold Brown at Patagonia. On the outskirts of town, Robins and Patterson were told that a forest ranger had been robbed of money and guns. They formed a posse and rode all night with no luck until a woman told them about two men down at Sonoita Creek. They caught the robbers and took them to Nogales.

In 1924, Sonoran farmers shipped 93 carloads of vegetables and melons north of the border. Wirt Bowman, who shipped garbanzos (chickpeas) to Spain through Nogales, served a term in the state legislature, acquired a Sonoran silver mine, remodeled the Montezuma Hotel, and acquired control of the Nogales

First National Bank. That same year, Nogales elected Attorney Duane Bird—son of Allen T. Bird, publisher of the *Oasis*—mayor and a slate of young Democrats to the council. This council framed a charter, which was adopted in 1926, to provide Nogales with a government that gave the town independence from the state.

Because of the terrible economic conditions in Mexico, Nogales was overrun with out-of-work Mexican laborers. To curb the influx of illegal entrants, the Immigration Service organized a department known as the Mounted Border Patrol. The Methodist minister Reverend O.A. Smith, who served his church in Nogales for more than 40 years, arranged with the Mexican government to take their citizens back to their homes for free.

The Nogales telephone line was extended to Patagonia and an automatic ringing device was installed. No longer did the operator have to keep hitting a lever to sound the bell until someone decided to answer the call. The Santa Cruz County board of supervisors still provided guards for patients with contagious

Mexico's president-elect Alvaro Obregón and Arizona's governor Thomas Campbell meet in Nogales. (Courtesy Pimería Alta Historical Society.)

121

diseases such as smallpox, who were housed in the lonely pest house on the road to Patagonia.

Hyman Capin, a native of Lithuania, arrived in the United States in the 1890s, first working in New York, then moving to El Paso and ultimately to Nogales. During the Revolution, Capin, a tailor by trade, made uniforms for the American officers and soldiers. After the Revolution, Capin closed his military tailoring shop and established the El Paso, a clothing store on Morley Avenue. Movie entertainment included *Robin Hood*, *The Gold Rush*, and *The Big Parade*. *The Phantom of the Opera*, accompanied by a special orchestra, played at the Nogales theatre. A guest lecturer, Vilhjalmer Stefansson, described his Arctic exploration to a rapt Nogales audience. By 1925, the economy was on the upswing and when metal prices rose, old mines were reopened and companies prospected for new ones.

The weekly *Nogales International* debuted under Craig Pottinger, who had worked for Hanson Sisk. Pottinger, born in Kentucky on June 30, 1891, started

Hyman Capin, pioneer Nogales tailor and merchant, shown here with son Harlan, opened the El Paso, a clothing store, after the revolution. (Courtesy Abe Chanin.)

The Hyman Capin family is a pioneer Nogales Jewish family whose contributions spanned the years from the Mexican Revolution to the present. (Courtesy Abe Chanin.)

his newspaper career in 1910 with the *Phoenix Gazette.* He was assigned to cover the Arizona statehood story and accompanied Arizona's first state Governor George W.P. Hunt down Washington Street on February 14, 1912. In Flagstaff, he founded the *Northern Arizona Leader.* An avid motorcycle enthusiast, he won several tournaments and wrote a column, "Pot-in-ginger." In 1923, he went to work for Sisk, but a year later, founded the *Nogales International,* whose editorials carried a strong Democratic slant. Even with Pottinger's railings against the dusty cow paths that passed for streets, it took Nogales three years before it let a contract for street paving. Often, he posted important national and local news on the wall outside his office as in the case of the end of World War I and the 1929 World Series scores on his bulletin board so that everyone might be informed. Pottinger borrowed a radio so passers-by could get play-by-play returns, seconds ahead of the wire service, thus scooping the *Herald.*

During the Six Week Revolution, Pottinger each day received a call from his friend in Naco to let him know that a bomber had taken off. About an hour later, the reporters would gather on Grand Avenue to watch the scene. Pottinger published the paper for 48 years and died at age 89 in 1980.

The Morgan brothers from Los Angeles bought out the Nogales-Tucson auto stage line and the road from Sonoita to Tucson was completed. In April 1926, Jack Johnson arrived in Nogales to train for his fight with Pat Lester in the Nogales Sonora bullring. On the day of the fight, special trains brought spectators from

Craig Pottinger, editor and publisher, founded the Nogales International, *a newspaper with a strong Democratic slant. (Courtesy Pimería Alta Historical Society.)*

Tucson, Phoenix, and Hermosillo. Johnson was named an honorary official of the Charleston dance held at the Nogales Theatre. John Summey, a handsome young man who became the Nogales postmaster in 1966, won the first prize at this dance.

Nogalians were proud enough to bust their buttons when a native son, Ralph O'Neill, returned home from World War I as an ace pilot. He served as General Director of the Mexican Air Service. The Hardy brothers, Charles and Leslie, both became Santa Cruz County attorneys. Their father, Justice of the Peace Charles Hardy, had once fined himself $10 for disturbing the peace. Born in Indian Fields, Kentucky, through their mother they claimed relationship with Daniel Boone. Both of the Hardy brothers received their law degrees from Wake Forest in North Carolina and went on to become Arizona judges.

There may be some truth to the old superstition that Ruby, a well-preserved ghost town a few miles north of Nogales, was cursed when a priest's grave was desecrated. This beautiful country has seen some of the worst violence in Santa Cruz County. In the 1870s, Jack Smith discovered rich ore reserves of silver, gold, lead, zinc, and copper at Ruby's Montana Mine. Smith was killed in his miner's shack by Apaches. Louis Zeckendorf sold the Ruby store to Julius Andrews for $900 and, in 1917, Andrews sold the store to Phil Clarke, who ran it while his wife taught school to the children of ranchers with the Arivaca Land and Cattle Company. Clarke's store prospered and the mines expanded. Times may have been good for Ruby, but they were desperate in Mexico. Clarke was never more than a step away from a gun. In 1920, the Clarkes moved to nearby Oro Blanco and leased the store to two brothers, John and Alex Frasier.

On February 27, two strangers entered the store. After he heard the cash register ring and then a gun shot, Clarke forgot about his guns and rushed into the store. Ezekiel Lara stood over the body of Alex Frasier with a smoking gun. After Lara and a companion forced Jack to open the safe, they took $200 and shot Jack in the eye before stealing $300 in merchandise and fleeing toward Mexico. When Joel Cuesta went to the store, he found the dead and dying Frasier brothers and notified the sheriff. Jack lived long enough to identify his assailants.

The Santa Cruz Supervisors offered a $1,000 reward for the capture of Lara, who had killed several Chinese in Mexico. Sheriff Earhardt, with posses from Santa Cruz and Pima Counties, took up the trail, but never caught the fugitives. Lara and Garcia returned to work in the mines south of Tucson, secure in the belief that they had left no witnesses. On a tip, Pima County Deputies Holliday and McClure went to arrest them. Garcia drew his gun and killed Holliday, but McClure killed him. Lara was never captured.

Frank Pearson bought the store from Phil Clarke, and on August 27, 1921, Pearson and his wife were shot and killed and Pearson's sister-in-law was wounded by bandits. Sheriff George White and Mr. and Mrs. George Camphius

This building, the Nogales Sonora Mexican Customs House, shown here in the 1930s, was demolished in 1962.

arrived on the scene. They could do nothing but clean up the bodies and take care of Pearson's four-year-old daughter. Camphius described the scene as "desolation beyond description." A neighbor identified the murderers as Placido Silvas and Manuel Martinez, who were last seen riding toward Mexico. They were extradited and tried in the United States where Silvas got life imprisonment and Martinez was sentenced to be hanged. On July 13, 1922, Sheriff George White and Deputy Leonard Smith put Martinez and Silvas, handcuffed to each other, in the backseat of White's car and set out for the state prison at Florence. Near Sahuarita, White's car turned turtle. He was killed in the accident and Smith was so badly injured that he died about a month later. Before his death, Smith testified that Martinez and Silvas had done nothing to cause the accident and that White, who was driving at high speed, had lost control of the car.

The Santa Cruz board of supervisors appointed Harry Saxon to serve out White's term. Within a week, Saxon caught a glimpse of Silvas in the mountains near the accident. Saxon's posse captured Martinez and Silvas, who offered no resistance. About 1,000 curious onlookers stared as Saxon and Quince Leatherman put the prisoners in jail. Martinez received a temporary stay of execution, but kept his destiny with death on August 10, 1923. Silvas escaped from the Florence penitentiary five years later and was never recaptured. In recent years it has been discovered that Silvas made his way back to Nogales, Sonora, where he lived for many years with his family.

Santa Cruz County Sheriff Raymond Earhardt led the search for Ezekiel Lara, who had robbed and shot the Frasier brothers.

Santa Cruz County Sheriff George White lost his life in a car accident while attempting to transport Placido Silvas and Manuel Martinez to the Arizona State prison in Florence. (Courtesy Pimería Alta Historical Society.)

In the mid-1920s, Clarke sold the Ruby store to a man named Worthington, who hid deserting African-American soldiers in the store. When the Arivaca military detachment learned of their whereabouts, they went after the fugitive soldiers with a barrage of bullets. Clarke threw Worthington out and closed the store. The Eagle Picher Company worked the mine from 1926 to 1949. Today, it is an interesting and well-preserved ghost town.

In 1926, matters came to a head between President Plutarcho Calles-Elías and the Roman Catholic Church. When Calles-Elías issued harsh edicts against the church, the priests closed down all churches in Mexico. Catholics attended services in Nogales, Arizona, after Nogales, Sonora's Purisima Concepción church served its last communion for several years. Twenty-eight Sisters of Mary fled the country to Nogales, Arizona where they built a novitiate and an academy for girls. When the Cristeros revolted into Mexico and the government committed horrible acts of suppression on Catholics, who appealed to the United States for help, President Calvin Coolidge sent Ambassador Whitney Morrow to attempt a reconciliation in 1927.

The Yaquis committed mayhem in northern Sonora in support of the Cristeros by destroying crops, damaging the railroads, and cutting off the water supply. To this day, only a few Roman Catholic orders are allowed to wear their habits in public in Mexico, and when the Pope visits Mexico, he receives special dispensation to wear his habit.

At Naco, rebel Catholic sympathizers under General Fausto Topete waged war against the federal garrison under the command of General Lucas Gonzalez. The rebels, who briefly controlled the northern Mexican states of Chihuahua, Sinaloa, and Sonora, wanted to reopen the churches. The siege of Naco began in late March of 1929 when the rebels loaded a railroad freight car with dynamite and sent it careening through Naco, Sonora. The car derailed and exploded before reaching its intended target, the center of town.

Mexicans dubbed the American mercenary pilots, who offered to fight with the rebels for a fee, the Yankee Doodle Escadrille. These pilots flew for the Mexican rebels for $250 per day, although it seems they rarely if ever got paid. These daredevil pilots included Patrick Murphy from Ardmore, Oklahoma; Commander "Colonel" Art Smith; George Koehler and B.M. Cole, both itinerant flight instructors from the Nogales, Arizona airport; and "General" R.H. Polk from Nashville. Before turning up in Arizona and Mexico, the cocky Patrick Murphy had been charged in Alabama with second-degree manslaughter after his mechanic died in a plane crash. Murphy himself had one leg badly crippled in the accident. On March 27, the Yankee Doodle Escadrille joined General Topete's forces in Agua Prieta just across the border from Douglas, Arizona.

Their bombs, which drifted across the border and dropped on Naco, Arizona, in flagrant violation of international treaties, put Washington, D.C. into a fair dither. President Herbert Hoover immediately sent troops to the border. Rebel planes, mostly U.S.-manufactured Stearman biplanes, were allowed to park on the Warren Ranch on the U.S. side of the border. The United Sates also provided Mexican federal troopers with American-made machine guns and ammunition. Lacking real aerial munitions, the Americans constructed fragmentation bombs from bolts, nuts, and pieces of scrap iron mixed with dynamite and bundled into suitcase-size leather bags. After they hand-ignited the strip fuse attached to the bag, the bombardiers quickly heaved the bomb out of the cockpit.

Rebel forces marched to Naco, surrounded the town, and dug in with their backs to the United States. Three days later, the rebels dropped leaflets over Naco, Sonora, warning of the imminent bombing. Koehler dropped four bombs that sprayed shrapnel on the U.S. side and killed two Mexican officers. When the first bomb dropped, Americans who had been enjoying the war in Naco bars caused a traffic jam trying to flee across the border.

Mercenary bombs were effective if launched properly, but wind played an important factor in determining where they landed. Before long, the Yankee Escadrille got pretty good at guessing where a bomb might hit. However, a few drifted over to the Naco, Arizona side and shattered windows, slightly wounded two Americans and two Mexican refugees, and blew up a Dodge car belonging to a Mexican officer who had stored it on the U.S. side for safekeeping.

On April 2, when two bombs from Murphy's plane fell on the U.S. side, an Ohio photographer and an Associated Press reporter suffered minor flesh wounds. Glass shattered in a grocery store, the Haas pharmacy, and the Phelps Dodge Mercantile. The AP correspondent reported that "the flier of the plane is an American with one leg and he is deeply sorry as are army officials." On April 3, a rebel monoplane dropped three bombs, one of which made a big hole in the ground on the American side. General Frank S. Cochiu, commander of the U.S. forces in Arizona, remarked, "Well, dirt is cheap." He paid Topete a visit and the general assured him that such a mishap would not happen again.

Early on the morning of April 4, the rebels dropped ten bombs. Murphy taunted the Federals by flying sideways and upside down with rebel bombardier Colonel Julio Ramirez in the back seat. Federal forces retaliated with bombing strikes from their black and orange Eaglerock biplane. Murphy's Travel Air took more than 30 hits before the engine quit. Murphy and Ramirez ejected safely, saluted the rebels, and hightailed it to Agua Prieta.

On April 6, Topete ordered an all-out attack on the Federal forces. Three rebel planes dropped bombs and rebel troops advanced behind three tractors that had been converted into army tanks. The Federals retaliated with a 1-pound cannon and with rifle fire. Around noon, a rebel plane dropped another bomb on Naco, Arizona. It exploded in the rear of Newton's Garage and slightly wounded George Newton.

U.S. military observers noted that crossfire ripped through Naco as though it were under attack. Residents sandbagged Naco buildings while dodging the whining bullets that ricocheted off buildings. During the Revolution, the

Pioneer aviator Patrick Murphy (left), one of the American mercenary pilots named the Yankee Doodle Escadrille, is pictured here with an unidentified friend. (Courtesy Ardmore Public Library, Ardmore, Oklahoma.)

Naco Hotel advertised bullet-proof rooms on its stationery. In the middle of an afternoon, rebel planes dropped more bombs from American airspace. U.S. infantry and artillery rolled into Naco, Arizona, and 18 airplanes from Texas patrolled American airspace with orders to shoot down any Mexican plane violating U.S. airspace.

On April 8, Murphy, along with Yankee Doodle Escadrille commander Art Smith, appeared at a news conference in Agua Prieta. Murphy said he did the stunts to show the Federals that he had no fear of them. Five days later, Topete's rebels had been cut down and rebel generals deserted their soldiers to the firing squads and headed across the border into the United States. When Topete walked across the border, Americans cheered him.

The Yankee Doodle Escadrille surrendered to U.S. authorities in Nogales, where they were arrested for violations of U.S. neutrality laws and held in the Santa Cruz County jail. Polk admitted that he did not care to be lined up against an adobe wall. None of the American aviators were ever prosecuted, but they complained about not being paid. It seems that a rebel treasurer absconded with their money and lit out for New York. Some said Murphy went to California or maybe China. No one is certain what happened to these intrepid pioneer aviators. The Yankee Doodle Escadrille has faded into oblivion, but they briefly held the nation's attention. Moreover, the Mexican Revolution demonstrated the importance of airplanes to the military.

Briefly, Camp Little revived when it received two troops of the all-black 10th Cavalry from Fort Huachuca and a battery of artillery joined the 650 infantrymen at the camp. From the safety of his suite at the Bowman Hotel, Abelardo Rodriguez, who had been taught in the Nogales High School by Ada EKey Jones and was now governor of Baja California, received news of the short-lived revolution. Rodriguez became President of Mexico in 1932.

During the abortive revolution, a frightened woman heard bombs dropping and died of a heart attack when she ran down a street. The Methodist ladies served a chicken pie supper that night. The Elks had arrived for a three-day convention and crossed the border to eat at La Caverna, but had to cut short their revelry because of a midnight curfew.

When the Mexican rebel officers saw that they were about to lose Nogales, Sonora, their last stronghold, they quit and asked for asylum in the United States. Although President Portes Gil announced the cessation of hostilities on May 1, 1929, there was more gunfire in Nogales that morning than at any time during the war. A stray machine gun bullet passed though the hood of a Buick sedan in Hank's Garage on Grand Avenue. Hank Myer, who owned the vehicle and was standing next to it at the time, kept the bullet for many years. After several hours, the Nogales rebels surrendered and the tricolor flag was raised over the Mexican custom house.

The year 1929 saw the closing of Camp Stephen Little. The Great Depression closed 13 banks and all Nogales city employees took a 15 percent pay cut. Works Project Administration funds provided for city and county improvements, along with the construction of a flood conduit through Ambos Nogales by the International Boundary and Water Commission in 1933, thus saving Nogales from total financial collapse.

Santa Cruz County Sheriff Harry. J. Patterson was one of the earliest sheriffs to make use of the airplane for searches. Born in Junction City, Texas, Patterson came to Arizona 1912 and later became a member of the Arizona Rangers. He married Mabel Sipe of Patagonia. In August of 1929, H.J. Johnston, contractor on the Nogales-Tucson highway, was shot and killed. About 30 minutes after the shooting, Sheriff Patterson arrested Dr. L.B. Pruitt, owner of a small Tubac ranch. Pruitt denied the shooting and said he offered to render first aid to Johnston, but was restrained from doing so. Two witnesses testified that they saw Pruitt leave Johnston's office after a single shot was fired. Pruitt admitted to arguing with Johnston over a $30 water bill, which Pruitt claimed the contractor owed him. During the trial, Johnston's friends filled the court roan and "glowered menacingly at Pruitt." The jury's verdict was "not guilty," probably because many considered the doctor "off-balance."

Nogales would enter the era of the Great Depression with serious economic problems, but with the diligence to grow, embrace progress, and succeed.

Santa Cruz County sheriff Harry J. Patterson was known as the flying sheriff because of his use of airplanes for searches.

131

11. THE GREAT DEPRESSION: 1929–1939

During the Great Depression, Nogales became a point where scores of Chinese were held until they could be sent back to China, putting an added strain on Santa Cruz County finances. Nogales took its place in aviation when it christened its tri-motored air transport, the *Greater Nogales*, at its airport

Every night, dozens of homesick out-of-work Chinese invaded Nogales by crawling under the border fence; in the morning, they asked for directions to the jail. When the jail had about 200 inmates, the Chinese were given a train ticket to San Francisco, where they were deported to China.

For three weeks, Nogales went without power because of a fight between the city council and the public utilities company. One by one, 13 banks were forced to foreclose on properties, including the Montezuma Hotel. Garages and service stations stopped extending credit. The city fathers cut employee wages and turned off the street lights at midnight. The relief kitchen, sponsored by the Knights of Pythias, served 378 meals during its first week of operation. Winter rains in 1931 ruined the tomato crop and summer rains helped the ranchers, but caused severe property damage.

In spite of protests from prominent citizens and legislators, Camp Stephen D. Little officially closed on May 5, 1933 and, by January of the following year, the trucks, horses, and mules had all left. Only three officers and a small contingent of African-American soldiers remained until the buildings were sold. On June 10, 1933, Congress combined the bureaus of immigration and naturalization into one organization, the United States Immigration and Naturalization Service. Its agents wore khaki uniforms and a few drove Model-T Fords, but where automobiles could not navigate the rugged terrain, the horse was still the transportation of choice. In the *Herald*, Craig Pottinger editorialized, "Headlines telling that millions or billions have been lost in the stock crash last month, terrorize a few people, but the ordinary run of humanity goes on about things as if nothing had happened."

Times were hard, but ranchers, who had great years because of heavy rains, donated beef, beans, and corn to the needy. The Works Project Administration built the Civic Building and made extensive public improvements. The International Boundary and Water Commission constructed a flood control conduit under Nogales, Arizona and Nogales, Mexico, saving both cities from total financial collapse.

Ambos Nogales still found ways to have fun. The two cities celebrated the 1930 Cinco de Mayo (5th of May) Fiesta, which everyone agreed was the best ever. On July 4, a team of daredevil pilots thrilled Nogales crowds with a flying exhibition. Betting ran heavy on the horned toad race and the winners of the baseball game received a $500 prize. The only disappointment came during a fight between a Mexican bull and an African lion that wanted nothing to do with the whole affair and ran away.

In August 1930, four Mexicans died in raging floods and damage to the two Nogales cities was estimated at $100,000. The Nogales police were frustrated when water stood 2 feet deep in the police station, but Louis Escalada and his friends had a high old time navigating Grand Avenue in a canoe. Several Nogalians learned to play polo and the sport caught on among the ranchers in southern Arizona. At Christmas time, the Nogales Rotary Club spent all of its money on food and clothing for the poor. The United States tightened immigration laws and the subsequent deportation of Mexican nationals to make more work for U.S. citizens caused some strain.

The produce industry did much to sustain both cities during this time. Audley Walter Cecil Holm was one of the first men to start a large-scale produce business in Nogales, along with his extensive export-import business. Born in Guatemala City, Guatemala on July 25, 1902, Walter was a son of Axel Christian Frederick

The Greater Nogales *was christened on May 17, 1931. (Courtesy Pimería Alta Historical Society.)*

Holm and Jesús Najarro. His father, a Danish naval officer, active in the music field, operated a Guatemala music store that sold instruments and musical materials. Walter attended Guatemala schools and graduated with the degree of Bachelor of Arts and Sciences from the Instituto Naciónal Central de Varones, part of San Carlos University in Guatemala. After working briefly for a coffee export company, he moved to Mexico City to study medicine. While attending classes, he worked for the Aguila Oil Company. Holm decided to embark on a business career in the United States and moved to Nogales in 1924, where he went to work for Roy & Titcomb. He worked for this firm for six years, first as a salesman and then as an estimator and purchasing agent.

In 1930, Holm entered the produce business, marketing vegetables grown in Mexico, and crossing the border at Nogales for distribution in the United States and Canada. He enlarged his business to include the prepackaging of tomatoes. A year later, a tomato grower in Los Mochis, Mexico, Martin Estrada, asked Holm to sell his tomatoes. Holm agreed and rented an office from Ray Sisk on the second floor of the *Nogales Herald* building. Business became all but impossible when the Mexican government nationalized all the produce-growing operations in Mexico and ordered that all produce be sold through one U.S. company, Wells Fargo.

Workers are packing and sorting tomatoes at the Holm Produce business in the 1930s. (Courtesy Pimería Alta Historical Society.)

This is a bird's-eye view of Nogales in the 1920s looking west from Nelson Avenue in Nogales, Arizona.

Holm married Mary Louise Oates, and one of their sons, Axel Christian Frederick, who continued in the produce business, now serves as president of the Pimería Alta Historical Society. When he could no longer sell produce, Walter moved the Holm family to Chicago where he sought work. He worked for a while for Riley and MacFarland, but then was once again forced to look for employment. The family moved to Mexico City where he found a job until Mexico denationalized the produce-growing operations and returned the business to growers who in turn resumed their normal selling connections in the United States.

While in Mexico City, Holm was befriended by a prominent Mexican military officer, General Juan Barragán, an aide to President Lázaro Cárdenas, who wanted Mexico to manufacture, not just assemble, cars. Holm traveled to Detroit in the summer of 1937 and researched the car manufacturing business for the Mexican government as Cárdenas's agent. Upon completion of that task, Holm returned to Nogales, bought into a Mexican produce company, and eventually bought a building that later became the site of the Arizona Bank.

In those days, green tomatoes, which had to be ripened later, were shipped by rail. Around 1944, Holm conceived of an idea of establishing a repacking plant for tomatoes. The green fruit, which had to be unloaded upon arrival by rail, was placed in ripening rooms to be gassed with ethylene to induce ripening. The fruit, sorted by size and color, was repacked in "boats" that held three to four tomatoes and then cellophane wrapped under the "Holm" label.

When people crossed the international border in the 1930s, they were questioned by personnel from three organizations: Immigration, Customs, and Agriculture. Today, these are combined into one operation.

Holm soon realized that he could get a better quality and better flavor tomato if the fruit could be left to ripen naturally on the vine. Vine-ripened fruit negated his huge investment in ripening and repacking, but he opted to persuade growers to ripen their fruit on the vine. This venture was risky, because the fruit had to be transported quickly by truck rather than the slower rail so that it would not spoil.

During hard times, crime rose. The first murder by a hitchhiker in Arizona occurred in 1933 near Nogales. George J. Shaughnessy, an 18-year-old New Yorker, shot and killed Lon Blankenship, a Tucson auto dealer. James V. Robins and G.A. Little represented Shaughnessy and Elbert R. Thurman prosecuted the case. Lawmen apprehended Shaughnessy at the Santa Rita Hotel in Tucson, where he confessed to shooting Blankenship when the victim resisted an effort to rob him of $325 and a watch.

Blankenship, who had picked up the hitchhiker on the outskirts of Nogales, like most people at the time, was not afraid of hitchhikers, most of whom had fallen on hard times and still had to get from one place to another. Six miles out of Nogales, Shaughnessy pulled a gun on Blankenship and when Blankenship tried to take the gun away, the hitchhiker shot him twice. He shoved Blankenship out of the car and then went to a home where he told a woman that he had found a wounded man and asked if she would take care of him. She agreed, but when he got Blankenship into the house, the wounded man said something in Spanish to the woman and she got scared and refused to have anything to do with the men.

Shaughnessy dragged Blankenship back inside the car and drove a few more miles before dumping his victim by the side of the road after promising to bring help. Judge Charles Hardy gave the youth every chance to change his plea to "not guilty" so he could have a jury trial, but Shaughnessy insisted he was guilty. Judge Hardy pronounced the death sentence and, on March 3, 1934, Shaughnessy met his fate.

The tragic murder of Nogales City Clerk Tracy Bird occurred when he came home early Sunday morning on October 16, 1938 after attending a dance. He was shot and killed in what appeared to have been a case of mistaken identity. His murderer, an African-American soldier, Frank Conner, was caught when he went to Carroon Mortuary looking for a doctor to take care of his injured hand and knee. Suspicious employees notified the sheriff's office, which arrested Conner and charged him with Bird's murder. At the trial, several witnesses testified that Conner had asked about a man named J.R. "Slim" Bird, who ran a café

Nasib Karam, member of a Nogales pioneer Lebanese family, became a Santa Cruz County attorney. (Courtesy Pimería Alta Historical Society.)

that catered to African-American soldiers. James Robbins argued that Conner intended to rob, but not to kill.

Nasib Karam polled the jury after they brought in the guilty verdict and on December 3, the death sentence was pronounced. Conner maintained a "jaunty disposition" throughout his trial, but broke down when his mother was led out of the courtroom. Karam, the son of a Lebanese immigrant who founded a Nogales Department store, went on to become a Santa Cruz County attorney and helped incorporate the town of Patagonia.

More people were driving cars and, unfortunately, automobile accidents were becoming more frequent. In 1930, Victor Wager and his first wife Ona de la Ossa were involved in an accident in which a Southern Pacific train just south of Tubac struck their car. Ona was killed instantly and Wager was so critically injured that he was not expected to live. He recovered and ran for Santa Cruz County sheriff, beating the very popular Pat Patterson.

Santa Cruz County Sheriff Victor Wager, born August 6, 1880 in Wager, Arkansas, moved to Prescott at the age of four and, by the time he was 12, was delivering mail between Prescott and Hilltop on a burro. Wager moved to Nogales, where he became county assessor in 1916. While Wager was sheriff, four prisoners broke out of the Santa Cruz County jail. The prisoners, who were quickly recaptured, had been taken to the yard for a sunbath because of an outbreak of influenza in the jail. They climbed on top of the disinfectant barrel, kicked a screen barrier loose, and jumped to the ground 16 feet below.

Sheriff John Jay Lowe, born March 5, 1852 in Tilden, Texas, arrived in Nogales in 1907 after a severe drought forced him out of the ranching business. That same year, he was named assistant to the Nogales City marshal and, a year later, was appointed deputy sheriff under Harry Saxon. Lowe claimed that his biggest headache was bootleggers. At age 76, he said, "I have never taken a life"

For Nogales, the trial of the decade was that of 66-year-old Louise Marshall, who admitted to shooting her husband Tom. Louise, a wealthy Tucson philanthropist, insisted that her husband Tom had been having an affair with their housekeeper Harriet Seymour and that the two of them had conspired to poison her. The trial was moved to Nogales because her attorneys felt that she could not get a fair trial in Tucson. Louise Foucar, born on May 31, 1864 in Boston, suffered in her youth from severe respiratory problems and her doctors recommended that she seek a drier climate. By 1898, when she arrived in Arizona, she had already earned two degrees from the University of Denver. She enrolled as a Botany graduate student at the University of Arizona and went on to become one of the first female professors at the University of Arizona.

On August 24, 1904, she married one of her students, Tom Keith Marshall. Marshall, born on a Kansas farm in 1879, worked as a farm hand and as a miner in Colorado before enrolling in the mining program at the University of Arizona in 1899. A year later, he took a class in geometry from Louise Foucar, for which he received a C grade. The early years of the Marshall marriage seemed happy enough. Tom was involved with mining, photography, the temperance movement,

Louise Foucar Marshall stood trial in Nogales for murdering her husband. (Courtesy Patricia Stephenson.)

and politics. Both Louise and Tom were interested in environmental issues and joined the Audubon Society. In the 1920s, Louise began buying property in the 900 block of East Third Street in Tucson, which still serves as home for the Marshall Foundation. The presence of Harriet Seymour, a widow, as housekeeper in the Marshall home took its toll on the marriage. Louise began to suffer severe stomachaches and suspected that her food was being poisoned. During the trial, Seymour denied all charges and disclaimed any affection for Tom or that she had clandestine relations with him.

In the early morning hours of April 27, 1931, Louise Foucar Marshall shot her husband four times with a pistol. She told a neighbor, "Mr. Marshall has been shot." An ambulance rushed Tom to the hospital, where he was operated on. When doctors saw that the operation was not successful, Tom was flown to a Los Angeles hospital where he died.

On September 13, 1931, Louise left with her housekeeper Mattie on the 60-mile, 2.25-hour trip from Tucson to Nogales where she would stand trial for murder. Louise and her entourage occupied ten rooms in the Bowman Hotel, which she described as "very comfortable." Harriet Seymour stayed at the same hotel as the jurors and the state's witnesses stayed at the Montezuma.

Tom Marshall was shot by his wife Louise in Tucson, Arizona. The trial was held in Nogales. (Courtesy Patricia Stephenson.)

The Honorable Judge William O'Connor presided over Louise Foucar Marshall's trial. O'Connor, born in San Mateo, California, had been appointed to the superior court in Santa Cruz County on October 20, 1913 by Arizona Governor George W.P. Hunt. He passed the bar in California, but moved to Nogales in 1900 where he taught school and was elected probate judge.

On trial for her life, Louise Foucar Marshall sat quietly and listened as the details of the shooting of her husband Tom were argued by the lawyers. She took the stand and told her side of the story. Dr. W.D. McNally, a Chicago toxicologist, testified that he had found dangerous amounts of arsenic in Louise's hair, and Dr. Charles J. Wilkerson admitted on the stand that he had treated Tom for a "social disease." Louise's defense team, including George Darnell, James P. Boyle, and Nogales attorney Duane Bird, successfully persuaded the jury that Tom Marshall died of a bungled surgery in Los Angeles that resulted in a post-operative infection, not from the bullet wounds.

The jury deliberated less than half an hour before returning a verdict and Judge O'Connor announced the verdict of "Not Guilty" to a cheering audience of mainly women. However, the vote took three ballots. The first ballot counted ten not guilty, two guilty, and imprisonment for life; the second ballot, eleven not guilty and one guilty with imprisonment for life; and the third and final ballot, twelve not guilty. Louise Foucar Marshall returned to Tucson and continued to support her favorite charities until she died at the age of 92 on July 10, 1956. During the ten-day trial, the courtroom had been packed and the hotels were full.

After the trial, Nogales returned to dealing with the problems of its everyday life. Roy & Titcomb's lumber mill was destroyed by a terrible fire and, after 30 years, its building shell was auctioned at a sheriff's sale. When the school board announced that the teaching staff would be reduced and no married women teachers would be hired, the hue and cry went up for the unfairness of the action. The *International* shrunk to six pages and Pottinger complained about merchants who spent nothing for advertising and then complained about poor business.

Nogalians were heartened by the win of President Franklin Delano Roosevelt in the presidential election and three Civilian Conservation Corps units were established in the Huachuca Mountains south of Patagonia. The defunct Camp Little now served as a home to 1,350 homeless transients, who were put to work moving sewer lines, doing advance work on the flood control project, and

Judge William O'Connor presided over the trial of Louise Marshall.

enlarging the airport runway. People found work through the National Recovery Act and Bracker's Army Store sold 2,000 sweaters to men in the transient camp. When the U.S. government offered to buy silver, the Montana mine at Ruby reopened. However, after years of heavy rains the cattlemen were in trouble once again because of a drought.

Nogales elected a mayor who managed to irritate a lot of people. Andrew Bettwy II, born in Altoona, Pennsylvania on September 24, 1894, received his early education in private German schools and was honorably discharged from the military in 1914 in Nogales. He stayed and located a ranch just outside of Nogales, and married Mary Chenoweth, the daughter of Dr. Harry K. Chenoweth. When he was elected mayor, Bettwy had already served as a state senator from Santa Cruz County in 1926 and 1928.

Bettwy began his mayoral term by firing 36 city employees and replacing them with 70 men of his choosing. Craig Pottinger started an "Oust Bettwy" campaign in the *International*. Bettwy responded by lowering the property tax rate

Andrew Bettwy II, a controversial Nogales mayor in the 1930s, began his term by firing 36 employees.

Following a severe drought in the 1930s, this Nogales train is caught in a flood. (Courtesy Pimería Alta Historical Society.)

and declaring a moratorium on the city's indebtedness. Nogales mayors served without pay, but Bettwy proposed that he should be paid $200 per month. The Valley National Bank sued Nogales for failing to pay its bills. All the state tax commissioner would say about the Nogales problem was, "an unusual situation exits here."

The terrible drought broke in August 1936 with a heavy downpour and, once again, the grass turned green and the cattle fattened. The Great Depression appeared to be coming to an end, and the Nogales city council had trimmed the budget and the payroll. City and county finances were in good shape. Construction on Mayor Bettwy's favorite project, the Nogales Civic Center, stopped because of unpaid bills and rumors that construction materials had disappeared. An investigation could not determine who was at fault, but the building was condemned before it was finished. By shoring up the walls, Nogales was able to use it as a warehouse.

In 1938, teachers once again received their pay in cash instead of cash warrants. In June, both Ambos Nogales cities paid homage to Father Louis Duval on the 50th anniversary of his priesthood. He had served as priest to the Sacred Heart Church since 1905 and had ministered to three generations of Nogalians as well as the Sonorans across the border.

When World War II broke out in Europe, the mines reopened in anticipation of the need for minerals and, for the first time in 20 years, the Trench handled ore from about 20 reactivated mines. The elegant Rancho Grande Hotel, which now housed Air Corps personnel, was renovated, and the Montezuma had a brand new ballroom and bar. Nogales, Sonora built several new nightclubs and a new bullring. A monument to Fray Marcos De Niza was built near Lochiel even

143

though no one can still agree on just exactly where the good friar crossed the border into the present-day United States. Both the United States and Mexico lowered tariffs on purchases, drawing retail trade from tourists across the border.

Nogales and the rest of the nation needed hope, and where better to get it than at the 1939 World's Fair in San Francisco? Nogales did not bother to conceal its pride when its very own Nogales Drum and Bugle Corps was chosen to appear at the Fair. The world's two largest bridges spanned San Francisco Bay and, to celebrate their completion, the world's largest man-made island rose from the waves. Mariners had long avoided the treacherous shoals just north of Yerba Buena Island, but now it was decided to create upon them the site of the Golden Gate International Exposition, to be known as Treasure Island. When the engineers finished, a 400-acre island appeared in the bay, connected by a 900-foot paved causeway to the Bay Bridge. Everywhere they went, the Drum and Bugle Corps flashed their smiles, strutted their stuff, and won the hearts of the people.

Dehlia Holler performed with the Nogales Drum and Bugle Corps at the 1939 San Francisco World's Fair.

12. The World War II Years and the Future

During World War II, trade with Mexico was drastically reduced, but many of its young men crossed the border to join the U.S. military. When news came of the bombing of Pearl Harbor, Nogales families listened anxiously for word of the Japanese bombing of the USS *Arizona*. Briefly, the United States closed the border and doubled the guards along the boundary.

Esther Ross Wray, who had originally christened the *Arizona*, now lived in Nogales where her husband had a business as a wholesale dealer in Mexican native artwork. Virginia Horrocks was the wife of Chief Gunner's Mate James William Horrocks, who served on the *Arizona*. On December 22, Horrocks, who had been in the Navy for 19 years, was officially declared Missing in Action. His wife had received a letter from him, postmarked December 2, stating that he expected war to break out any minute. Eventually, he was declared dead.

When the United States declared war on Japan, the United States–Mexico Joint Defense Commission formed and, for the duration of the war, "dissolved" the border. Both Mexico and the United States had vested interests in keeping the border safe. Three days after the Pearl Harbor bombing, 900 Mexican troops arrived in Nogales, Arizona just before midnight and boarded a special train with their horses, ammunition, and trucks to guard the Pacific coast. The American consul invited the Mexican officers to a banquet at La Caverna Restaurant across the border. Fort Huachuca troops arrived to guard the Nogales reservoirs, the pumping plant, and the electric power station.

The U.S. Immigration and Naturalization Service received its first airplane in 1941, along with four-wheel drive vehicles and one-way radio communication. The Border Patrol agents escorted Japanese prisoners to internment camps, guarded German prison camps within the United States, and arrested draft dodgers, or "slackers" as they were known. Border Patrol agents became experts at reading signs and tracks indicating a disturbance, such as a footprint or an overturned rock. Slackers often crossed into Mexico to escape the draft.

Housewives saved aluminum foil and fat, and learned government regulations regarding the rationing of tires, gasoline, sugar, coffee, and shoes. Scrap metal drives were good excuses for picnics and other festivities. The old Titcomb foundry turned out parts for the Consolidated Vultee aircraft company in Tucson. The *International* advertised War Bond Rallies, honored President Franklin D. Roosevelt on his birthday, and mourned his death in 1945. By 1944, more than 1,400 Santa Cruz residents were serving in the Armed Forces. Forty-three had either been killed or were missing in action. On August 17, three days after President Harry S. Truman announced the end of World War II, Ambos Nogales put on a huge Peace Parade.

After the war, men who had trained in southern Arizona returned to enjoy the balmy winter climate. Tourists once again streamed across the border to buy curios and dine at the elegant Caverns, which was destroyed in the 1970s by fire. Nogales remained a free port and a third gate was added to take care of trucks crossing the border. Unlike many communities, Nogales saw unparalleled prosperity after the war. The Valley National Bank bought the First National Bank. Produce shipments increased.

William Beatus bought the Rancho Grande Hotel and developed a tract of expensive homes overlooking the city. When runway lights were finally installed at the airport, Beatus scared the wits out of Nogalians by zooming over the city after dark. A small factory made reeds for musical instruments and musical instrument makers, including Artley Flutes, set up plants in Nogales. The music makers were followed by companies like Samsonite and by electronics firms, such as Motorola. Assembly plants were in Nogales, Sonora, while the preassembly and warehousing was done in Arizona. These were the first *maquilladoras,* or "Twin Plants."

William Beatus purchased the elegant Rancho Grande Hotel during the prosperous post-war years that Nogales enjoyed.

Obregón Street in Nogales Sonora is a popular shopping area for visitors from north of the border.

In 1946, John Wayne and the cast of *Red River*, which was being filmed near Elgin, attended a rodeo at Sonoita. Three thousand people enjoyed a barbecue financed by the film company. Other Nogales movies from that era included *David and Bathsheba*, starring Gregory Peck and Susan Hayward, and *Broken Arrow*, starring Jeff Chandler. Jim Frazier, the unofficial mayor of Elgin, had the part of a trapper in the epic *Red River*, the story of the first cattle drive over the old Chisholm Trail.

Once again, both Nogales cities were visited by a Mexican president, Miguel Alemán, the son of a revolutionary general of the same name. Alemán's administration fostered a revival of economic growth and new public works, including dams, highways, and schools like the new National University, came into being.

In 1947, Walter Holm launched a fleet of trucks to bring Mexico's produce directly to his Nogales warehouse dock. The Nogales Airport went international when it became the terminus for the Aeronaves de Mexico. Except for beef, importers thrived in 1948. Hoof and mouth disease had broken out in the interior of Mexico and no cattle could be shipped into the United States. Patagonia became the second town in Santa Cruz County to incorporate, with grocer William Waggoner as mayor. As early as 1947, Sheriff John J. Lowe had called attention to the border narcotics problem. The notorious Purple Gang of Detroit tried to set themselves up as ranchers near the border. Lowe thought that the underworld had their representatives in Mexico to plant and cultivate opium and to process the drug.

Mexico's president Miguel Alemán visits Nogales, Arizona and Mexico. (Courtesy Pimería Alta Historical Society.)

In 1948, Ada EKey Jones, Joseph Wise, former Nogales Mayor Harry J. Karns, and Nogales *Herald* editor Hanson R. Sisk formed the Pimería Alta Historical Society to preserve the rich history of the area. Harry Karns, a one-time mayor of Nogales, was born in Jamestown, New York on May 17, 1880. Karns, interested in mining and engineering, arrived in Nogales in 1907. He worked in Mexico's mines and established a mercantile in Nogales, Arizona. Two years later, he opened the Karns Terminal Bonded Warehouse. In 1914, Karns was elected to represent Santa Cruz County in the Arizona state legislature. From 1920 to 1922, he served on the Nogales city council and helped draft Nogales's first city charter.

As a student of Arizona history, Karns translated the diary of Captain Juan Mateo Manje, who accompanied Padre Eusebio Kino on his explorations in the Pimería Alta. In 1934, when Karns found business slack and was retiring as mayor, he became determined to be more than an armchair historian. Over a period of two years, he covered most of the places mentioned by Kino and Manje.

In January 1949, Santa Cruz County experienced three heavy snowstorms and ice floated down the Santa Cruz River. With rail transportation disrupted for several weeks, Walter Holm brought tomatoes out of Mexico by airplane. A city sales tax was adopted during Mayor Jose Colunga's administration. Under Mayor Abe Rochlin (1959–1965) Nogales adopted its first zoning ordinance and new construction included a public swimming pool, St. Joseph's Hospital, and the Meadow Hills Golf Club, along with the dedication of the Nogales Public Library.

In 1950, Nogales's steadily declining population began to reverse. People found plenty of work in the produce and hotel industries, and the million-dollar Fray Marcos de Niza Hotel opened. However, passenger rail service between Nogales and Tucson stopped in 1951. A year later, the Frank Reed School for African-

Gregory Peck is pictured here on the set of Bathsheba, *one of many films produced in Nogales. (Courtesy Pimería Alta Historical Society.)*

American students closed and the students and teachers were assimilated into the public elementary school system. The school had been named for Frank Reed, a black soldier stationed at Camp Little.

In 1953, a petite, beautiful blonde lady from South Bend, Texas took southern Arizona by storm. Patricia McCormick, a student of art and opera, professionally fought the bulls in the Nogales, Sonora bullring. Seat prices depended on whether one sat on the sunny side or shady side of the ring. She was feted by the Tucson media. During her fight, she wrapped the bull around her while never retreating as she performed intricate cape passes in her Andalusian suit. Fans were pleased with her fight and a jewelry store in Nogales, Arizona reopened on Saturday night afterwards so she could choose a gift. She wanted a medal, but her manager suggested a watch because she was frequently late. McCormick went on to fight the bulls in Mexico City and Portugal.

In 1953, Patricia McCormick captured the hearts of Ambos Nogales when she fought the bulls in Nogales, Sonora.

During this decade, duty collections reached $1 million. With the desire to put the organization in a more favorable light, U.S. Customs officers were unofficially designated as greeters and stopped wearing guns. Over the years, there had been a number of gun accidents within the Customs organization. When Luke Short fired at his tied horse, a bullet ricocheted through a Customs outhouse where a clerk was reading a newspaper. Joe Sorrells died of a bullet that accidentally hit the Nogales guardhouse. Inspector Charley Jones fired on a robber who tried to flee across the border after he made an unsuccessful attempt to rob Espinosa's Money Exchange.

On December 4, 1958, in a story unusual for southern Arizona, three Tucson Boy Scouts, missing since November 15, were found frozen to death on a snow-covered peak in the rugged Santa Rita Mountains. Mike Early, Michael La Noue, and David Greenberg, who had become separated from their companions, died around what appeared to be the site where they made an attempt to start a fire. Santa Cruz Deputy Sheriff Jack Sullivan sent prearranged smoke signals to announce that he had found the boys. Judge Oliver Rothrock, with County Attorney James Hathaway, rode horseback to the scene to conduct an inquest and give permission to remove the bodies to a Tucson mortuary. Helicopters, small planes, bloodhounds, special rescue dogs, and 700 men participated in the sad search.

In 1959, Howard Inches from Miami, Florida purchased the Rancho Grande Hotel. Inches, who produced supplemental health foods, conducted a summer school attended by students from all over the United States. They exercised, ate healthy diets, attended lectures, and toured the Buena Vista Ranches, which had also been bought and subdivided by Inches. Several students invested in building lots, but never received deeds to their property. Eventually, Inches was arrested for fraud and acquitted in Arizona, but convicted in California. The elegant old hotel was sold for taxes and razed in 1967.

By the mid-1960s, the international gate spanned a nine-lane entrance. In 1966, the Nature Conservancy purchased a large tract of land on Sonoita Creek that became internationally famous with bird watchers. That same year, Interstate Highway 19 entered Nogales, which contributed to the development of the Twin Plants. U.S. Customs officers began carrying arms again and became involved in an offensive against marijuana smugglers. A bracero program, which processed Mexicans who wanted to work in Arizona, Arkansas, Idaho, and Colorado, closed in 1962.

The year 1974 saw another visit by U.S. and Mexican presidents to Nogales. President Gerald Ford, with Mexico's President Luis Echeverría, and Secretary of State Henry Kissinger, met as a demonstration of good will. In 1976, construction started on the Smithsonian Astrophysical Observatory on Mt. Hopkins, the second highest peak in the Santa Ritas. Five years later, it had become the Smithsonian's largest field facility.

The search for 50-year-old Maurice Powell ended on October 10, 1961, when the bullet-ridden body of the crippled prospector was found. Powell had

U.S. President Gerald Ford appeared with Mexican President Luis Echeverría and Secretary of State Henry Kissinger in 1974. (Courtesy Pimería Alta Historical Society.)

befriended two men, Ronald Goodyear and Steven Jackson. They told Santa Cruz Deputy Sheriff Joe Hill, who caught them driving Powell's truck, that they could not remember where Powell had gone. Deputies found several guns and knives and Hill arrested them for carrying concealed weapons. Goodyear and Jackson, when told that Powell's body had been found, confessed. A year earlier, Goodyear had been placed in the California State Hospital as a sexual deviate. Here he met Jackson and they planned, upon their release, to come to Arizona and prospect. They met Maurice "Shorty" Powell and the three of them moved to the Mowry area. On October 5, after the three men had several drinks, Jackson staggered home hysterically crying "It's done and I'm glad." Outside, Goodyear saw that Powell had been murdered. They disposed of the body near the World's Fair mine, after robbing Powell of $80. The defense, in hopes of getting a lenient sentence, struck all men from the jury, but the all-woman jury brought in a verdict of guilty with a recommendation for the death penalty. However, a mistrial was declared and, over the years with many of the principals no longer available, the case against Goodyear and Jackson was plea bargained to a prison sentence.

During the February 1971 jail riot, Santa Cruz County Sheriff Zeke Bejarano faced a serious problem. The dungeon-like stone jail, built in 1903, had corroded metal cells that were so decomposed that the prisoners tore off strips to make knives. Bejarano held federal prisoners in the county jail until they could be transferred to other facilities. All prisoners were put in one tank. Hardcore felons could not be separated from Saturday night drunks and kids overstaying their Mexican work permits. Rioters set fire to the jail roof, burning out the superintendent of education's office above it. Then they barricaded cell doors. When Bejarano forced the door open, a spear-shaped piece of pipe narrowly missed his head.

In 1977, Santa Cruz County Sheriff Jaime Teyechea brought 31 years of experience as a lawman to the department. Three days after his discharge in 1945, he had been hired by J.J. Lowe as a deputy. While working for the Nogales Police Department, he took out a personal loan to purchase uniforms and his colleagues paid him a little each month until their uniforms were paid off. Teyechea, a zone commander for five counties while working for the Arizona Department of Public Safety, worked six days a week and, on his day off, maintained his car and caught up on paperwork. When he took over the sheriff's department, Teyechea organized the office along semi-military lines and petitioned the supervisors for more equipment and money to send officers to training programs. Teyechea, urging the county to purchase a back-up generator for the jail, warned, "When the power goes off there is no lighting and in a short time things become very dangerous." Teyechea saw law enforcement changes from the 1940s through the 1980s before he retired in Nogales.

Travis Edmonson, a popular Nogales balladeer, topped the charts along with his partner Oliver "Bud" Dashiel. (Courtesy Travis Edmonson.)

In the 1960s, Nogales's own Travis Edmonson, with his partner Oliver "Bud" Dashiel rode to the top of the national music charts with their folk music. Travis sang in St. Andrew's Episcopal Church in Nogales, Arizona and in La Caverna restaurant in Nogales, Sonora. His father was a long-time pharmacist born on the Mexican side of Aguas Calientes and his mother taught school for many years in Nogales. While at the University of Arizona, Travis worked on a Spanish-Yaqui dictionary and was made an honorary member of the tribe in 1948. After a stint in the military, he teemed up with Bud Dashiel and their music struck a chord in the hearts of their audiences. Since 1982, when Travis suffered from an aneurysm and a stroke, he has not been able to play the guitar. Ironically, his partner Bud Dashiel died in the 1980s of a brain tumor. Recently, a compact disc of Travis's most popular songs has been released.

Given Santa Cruz County's proximity to the border, international trade, *maquiladora* manufacturing, produce, and tourism have evolved as the most successful modern industries. Nogales is one of the largest crossing points for fresh produce in the United States, with more than 4 billion pounds of fruits and vegetables shipped across its border each year. As Arizona's largest Mexican port of entry, Nogales accounts for two-thirds of all commercial traffic entering Arizona from Mexico. According to U.S. Customs, approximately 180,000 commercial trucks cross the Nogales border each year and that number is growing. Each year, more than $1 billion worth of Mexican produce passes through Nogales bound for Canada and the United States. Approximately 1,300 trucks from Mexico enter Nogales every day during the produce transport season, which runs from November through May. When the 1994 implementation of the North American Free Trade Agreement opened the door for free trade, Nogales, Arizona and Nogales, Sonora became major international trade centers.

Assembly plants, known as *maquiladoras*, take advantage of inexpensive Mexican labor to create finished products from parts shipped in from around the world. Nogales, Arizona-Sonora is home to one of the largest twin plant programs along the U.S.–Mexican border. The Twin Plant Program allows American companies to transport their unassembled parts, raw materials, and components into Mexico duty-free and exempt from many Mexican tariffs and import restrictions. Border crossings between twin plants are generally expedited by customs officials of both countries and are complemented by the most modern custom brokerage firms along the U.S.–Mexican border. Twin plants on the Arizona side typically function as administrative and distribution facilities and on the Mexican side, frequently manufacture or assemble parts or components, where greater precision, security, or worker skills are necessary.

On July 8, 2002, a black day in Tubac, the Tubac Presidio, Arizona's oldest state park, closed temporarily for lack of funds. The cannon was fired as the color guard marched to the base of the flag pole. With "Taps" playing in the distance, the flag was lowered and now lies on a table waiting to be unfurled.

On Thursday, June 26, 2002, Mayor Abraham Zaied of Nogales, Sonora called Mayor Marco López seeking help as a result of a severe drought that was drying

Nogales, Arizona mayor Marco Lopéz became the youngest mayor in the state in 2000. (Courtesy mayor's office.)

up the Nogales, Sonora water wells. In May, the Nogales, Sonora water wells had begun to go dry and the city could no longer offer a traditional service of giving away water to the poor. A month later, three more wells ran dry and water delivery stopped to those neighborhoods that had no running water. In the neighborhoods with running water, service was limited to a couple of hours a day. Mayor López, the city council, and administration acted quickly to help Nogales, Sonora. Both governments activated their bi-national emergency response plan and agreed that Nogales, Arizona would charge Nogales, Sonora $1.80 for every 1,000 gallons of water used. A temporary water line was connected near the Dennis DeConcini Port of Entry so that Mexican water tankers could fill up and deliver water to thousands of families in Nogales, Sonora. For over a week, thousands of people in Sonora had not received a drop of water.

In 2000, Nogales, Arizona elected the youngest mayor in the state's history, 22-year-old Marco Lopéz, who adopted the United States as his philosophical ground and as his home in 1994. While working as a page for Congressman Ed

Pastor in the U.S. House of Representatives, he became determined to obtain the best possible education. In 1996, he became the first student to enroll in the University of Arizona's Arizona International College and graduated with a Bachelors Degree in Liberal Arts and Political Science in 1999. Although Lopéz chose the United States as his home and his future, his ties to Mexico are strong. He views the border issues as vital and immigration as more than just policy—it is people with faces, names, and talents.

Nogales, Sonora, on the other hand, elected Mayor Abraham Zaied Dabdoub. Zaied, born in Bethlehem, speaks Spanish with an Arabic accent. The 63-year-old Zaied moved with his family to Mexico when he was 12 years old. A descendant of Palestinian Catholics, he married a local Mexican woman, Alma Araiza. After taking one term off, as required by the Mexican constitution, Zaied ran for a second term of mayor in 2000. Both mayors reflect life on the border, although they are vastly contrasting in age and education. They show how people can work together even across borders.

Cabot Sedgwick, longtime Nogalian and avid keeper of the area treasures, takes pride in the city of Nogales. (Courtesy Tucson Citizen.*)*

BIBLIOGRAPHY

Bailey, L.H., ed. *The A.B. Gray Report*. Great West and Indian Series XXIV, Western Series II. Los Angeles: Westernlore Press, 1963.

Brownell, Elizabeth R. *They Lived in Tubac*. Tucson: Westernlore Press, 1986.

Cleaveland, Norman and George Fitzpatrick. *The Morleys: Young Upstarts on the Southwest Frontier*. Albuquerque: Calvin Horn Publishing, Inc., 1971.

Dreyfus, John J., Ed. *A History of Arizona's Counties and Courthouses*. Tucson, Arizona: Arizona Historical Society, 1972.

Hall, et al. *Drawing the Borderline: Artist Explorers of the U.S. Mexico Boundary Survey*. Albuquerque: The Albuquerque Museum, 1996.

Hall, Linda B., and Don M. Coerver. *Revolution on the Border: The United States and Mexico, 1910–1920*. Albuquerque: University of New Mexico, 1988.

Hallenbeck, Cleve. *The Journey of Fray Marcos de Niza*. Dallas: University Press, 1949; new ed., Dallas: Southern Methodist University Press, 1987.

Johnson, William Weber. *Heroic Mexico*. Garden City, NY: Doubleday & Company, Inc., 1968.

Officer, James E., Meredith Schuetz-Miller, and Bernard L. Fontana, eds. *The Pimería Alta: Missions & More*. Tucson: Southwestern Mission Research Center, Inc., 1996.

Polzer, Charles W. *Kino Guide II: His Missions—His Monuments*. Tucson: Southwestern Mission Research Center, Inc., 1998.

Ready, Alma. *Nogales Arizona: 1880–1980 Centennial Anniversary*. Nogales: Pimería Alta Historical Society, 1980.

————. *Open Range and Hidden Silver: Arizona's Santa Cruz County*. Nogales: Alto Press, 1973.

Riley, Caroll L. "Road to Hawikuh: Trade and Trade Routes to Cibola-Zuni during Late Prehistoric and Early Historic Times." *Kiva* 41 (Winter 1975).

Rodack, Madeleine T., ed. and trans. *Adolph F. Bandelier's The Discovery of New Mexico by the Franciscan Monk, Friar Marcos de Niza, in 1539*. Tucson: University of Arizona Press, 1981.

Rochlin, Fred and Harriet. "The Heart of Ambos Nogales" *Journal of Arizona History* 17 (2) Tucson, 1976.

Stewart, Janet Ann. *Arizona Ranch Houses: Southern Territorial Styles, 1867–1900*. Tucson: University of Arizona Press, 1987.

INDEX

This happy tourist in Nogales, Sonora probably enjoyed a dinner at the Caverns and shopping on Obregón Street.